E·
I Ha

D1388321

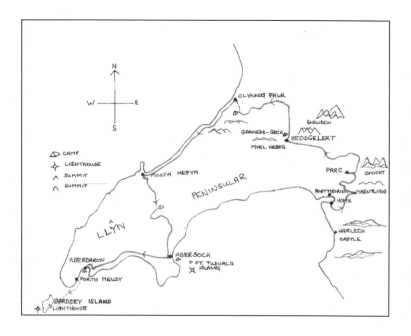

OWAIN HUGHES

Everything
I Have Always Forgotten

SEREN

Seren is the book imprint of
Poetry Wales Press Ltd.
57 Nolton Street, Bridgend, Wales, CF31 3AE

www.serenbooks.com
facebook.com/SerenBooks
Twitter: @SerenBooks

The right of Owain Hughes to be identified as
the editor of this work has been asserted in accordance
with the Copyright, Designs and Patents Act, 1988.

© Copyright Owain Hughes, 2013

ISBN 978-1-78172-099-8
Mobi 978-1-78172-100-1
Epub 978-1-78172-101-8

A CIP record for this title is available from the British Library.

All rights reserved. No part of this publication may be reproduced,
stored in a retrieval system, or transmitted at any time or by any means,
electronic, mechanical, photocopying, recording or otherwise without
the prior permission of the copyright holder.

*The publisher acknowledges the financial assistance of the Welsh Books
Council.*

Printed by Bell and Bain Ltd., Glasgow

CONTENTS

Introduction 7

PART I – THE BEGINNING

I Leftovers of the 1920s 13
II The First Winters 18
III Home 26
IV The House 33
V Fireside Tales 45
VI Postwar Survival / Babysitters 56
VII Granny Cadogan 66
VIII Nice Sicilian Murderer 71
IX Berserk Jeep Hits London 80
X Dylan 91
XI Back to W.W.II 99
XII Haven with a Spy 103
XIII Rain, Sex, School 109
XIV Misty Mountain 115
XV Mountains and Guns 125
XVI The Sailing Bug 133
XVII Now Hooked on Sailing 139
XVIII Pony Trekking 150
XIX A Shepherd Swims 156
XX My Very Own Trip 161
XXI Courting Death on Cliffs 166

PART II – THE JOURNEY

XXII The Flying Dutchman 177
XXIII The Journey Begins 185
XXIV The Journey Blessed 199
XXV Into the Wild 204
XXVI Merlin and Other Wizards 209
XXVII Passage To Bardsey 218
XXVIII Storm Bound 223
XXIX Home At Last 230

Afterword 233

INTRODUCTION

As Mother lay dying, crippled by pain and humiliated by incapacity, I asked her if she was worried about me when I walked to Bardsey Island with my school friend Alan, at the age of eleven. She closed her eyes and scrunched up her deeply lined face with concentrated thought. After a while, without opening her eyes, she said only: "I forget" and her face relaxed again, relieved not to have to try to remember any more. I had waited too long to ask. The smell of aseptic old people's home flooded back over my old memories of young health and strength, hiking in those clean mountains, now that I was forty...

Rarely do I talk of, or seek to remember, my childhood. Those who knew my circumstances say that it must have been 'idyllic', but childhood is often pain and simple sadness. It is lost, as if shrouded in the clouds that hang about the summits of mountains. From time to time, those clouds may be rent with a tear, opening up a view of the landscape, oh so far, far below – or showing in this simile, just for one moment in time, a brief historical vignette. These are some such brief glimpses through the clouds that I shall try to show you, piece by piece. Perhaps they are not special, but they are mine. Though some of what I relate derives from the tales of others, even some of my own, I confess that many may be apocryphal – but what would be the interest in two people telling the same story? It would be mere repetition worthy of a parrot or a tape-recorder, not a large and creative family.

Bardsey was my first self-motivated trip in 1955. Of course, by then I had travelled by train alone to school, starting at the age of seven, but that was not my choice. Neither was the expedition which my youngest sister and I undertook on horseback. The true revelation came when I decided where I wanted to go. When I walked to Bardsey, financing the trip myself... that was the real beginning of my life. That led to 1963 (aged nineteen), when I walked and hitchhiked to the south of Iran, then across the Sahara, from Mauritania to Egypt. These were true expressions of choice. As politics have panned out, many of those trips could hardly be made today, as I made them then: with a backpack, a sleeping bag, a notebook and phrasebooks of Farsi, Arabic, Turkish and Greek. The trip to Bardsey was the last time I ever brought a tent. A tent is too great an advertisement of where one is sleeping. Of course, being eleven years old, Alan and I were insouciant, totally unaware of risk from other human beings. We were accustomed to the kindness and sharing that had sprung from the common suffering of the appalling Second World War. The war in which everyone was defeated except the Americans. Later I was to learn that better by far is to creep into the shelter of a bridge or unused drainage pipe after dark and there to simply slip into the sleeping bag, to rest unbeknownst to the world in general and the local populace in particular. Oh yes, Alan and I certainly respected cliffs, tides and heavy storms at altitude or at sea – but 'Evil-Doers' were not in our lexicon, as they surely would be today.

As for training my Parents to allow me such liberty, it seemed to come to them quite naturally and, besides, I was the fifth child so I have my older siblings to thank for laying the groundwork, for raising our Parents so well and so liberally...

Before I could walk and climb, I had to crawl, so I quote the bard, Mr Thomas: "Let us begin at the beginning."

This is a tale of a child's life before the concept of 'Helicopter Parents' became so pervasive: those parents who continually hover over their offspring, watching that no harm could possibly befall their precious babies, their fledglings.

Before the Padded, Insulated, Protected – the 'Bubble-Wrapped' World came into existence. I was raised under Father's principle of: "plenty of benign neglect". Indeed, he himself had been raised by his widowed mother and spinster aunts and became obsessed with their cloying, over-protective care. He essentially left home at the age of sixteen.

So, I was always fed, had a roof over my head, was somewhat clothed, sent to private schools and my reports were read and remarked upon. With any more supervision than that, exactly what encourages a child to develop?

Recently, I heard that a friend's young teenage daughter had disappeared after a quarrel with her parents over her privacy from her three younger brothers. Desperate after searching for three hours, they called their neighbours – one of whom was the village mayor. It was a cold, drizzling, winter's day in this southern French village and night would soon be coming on. Their friend and neighbour, the mayor, told them that after three hours' absence, he was obliged by law to call in the police. After dark, they would have to call in a helicopter. *Gendarmes* and CRS officers, twenty vehicles full, combed the surrounding area until finally a tracking dog was brought from 100 kilometres away. The dog immediately found the child cowering under a bush in her parents' very garden.

As a toddler, I wore a little harness with round bells on it, so that Mother knew just where I was as I tinkled about like a little goat... oh the joy of cantering off alone amongst the gorse bushes, out of sight of authority! Mother never held the reins (I probably pulled at them too much, like an untrained dog on a leash), yet I was tagged as surely as if I wore a GPS microchip. Once I grew out of that harness, I could disappear in a rage or a mood and no one would notice I was gone. I would come home when I was hungry, cold and wet. True Refugees do not have the luxury of sulking.

So begins the unfolding of my life, like a snail, spiralling out and out and suddenly on and on into the great unknown to be discovered. Other places, other times – we start at point zero, and adventure, eventually, to the uttermost corners of the earth, but it is a spiralling thing that develops and finally spins out on its own – this is Life.

PART 1

THE BEGINNING

I

LEFTOVERS OF THE 1920s

Oh, that delicious first moment of six-year-old conscious-ness in the morning: when the bedroom wall is dappled by limpid sunlight, so clear and fresh, filtering through tree leaves that shiver slightly in the early morning breeze – their blurred shadows flickering and dancing upon the wallpaper by my bed. That delicious, warm first moment when there is a tremor in one's lower self and, since Mother is not there to say: "No wigwig", one can indeed indulge in secret, delicious, forbidden wigwig. It could have gone on for ever and ever, but...

I heard the growl of a lorry outside and, even forgetting wigwig, sat up and looked out of the window. There was an old lorry in the garden outside, towing away Father's 1922 two-seater Bentley. It looked short and squat with its great barrel of a hood, held in place by a heavy leather girth and buckle – big and powerful as a steam locomotive to my child's eyes. It stood high and ungainly on its huge wheels, more like a motorized carriage than a car... wasn't it Etore Bugatti who once declared: "Mr Bentley builds the fastest trucks on the road today"? Only the day before, I had been playing in it where it stood in a stable, covered in chicken shit, its tyres flat, its windshield yellow from the ageing of the layer of plastic in the 'sandwich' that was Triplex glass. It had been stored there throughout the great uncertainty of the Second World War. Now, ignominiously, the noble touring car was being dragged from its geriatric roost amongst the chickens, past the huge, stark ruins of the medieval castle that stood in jagged dilapidation in the garden: decayed, cavity-riddled fangs of former medieval military might. And now our beloved Benty was gone…

A few years later, I discovered the enormous leather suitcases that were custom-made for the luggage rack of that car. There were two of them, almost one and a half metres long and quite shallow – so one could lay out a full ball gown or suit of tails in one without folding or creasing them. I also found Father's motoring clothes, worthy of a First World War fighter pilot: an ankle-length, tight-waisted white leather greatcoat, with elbow-length gauntlets and helmet to match. Hardly practical attire for getting in and out of a little bi-plane, or even a motor car, for that matter. He must have cut quite a figure driving his gleaming, dark green, 3.5 litre two-seater Bentley, tall and slim as he was then, the brilliantly successful, the lionized young novelist that he was, with a dark beard and such a romantic air – that first time in 1931 when he went to stay with Mother's family in their country mansion.

Father was discovered there prowling around upstairs by a Bavarian cousin, a Baroness Pia von Aretin (who later helped him enormously with his last novel by introducing him to people who had known Hitler when he was on the lam after the failed Munich Putsch) pacing the corridors of my grandmother's house, barefoot. Naturally, being a well-bred German girl, she waited for him to introduce himself, but all he said was: "Do you speak Chinese?" Of course, his romantic, creative, exotic aura was given another lift. Then, when he went to change for dinner, the valet had laid out a tent for him on his bed! He rang for the valet and asked about his tent: "Well sir, we found not a single bag in your motor, all we could find was the tent and seeing as we'd heard in the servants' hall that you'd been to Arabia and such foreign parts, we thought perhaps that you might be in the habit of wearing tribal robes instead of trousers and tails." The aura gained yet another tone of intensity. Mother's family was at once impressed by his fame, but fearful of the scandalous controversy around his first novel. That children could be such wicked little savages when left to themselves – not the 'little angels' brought downstairs by nurses, washed, combed and forced to behave. 'His' children managed surprisingly well in the captivity of pirates, much as Golding's boys later survived on a desert island. Children are not by nature innocents; they are already learning survival techniques.

What a time-warp the Second World War created! Before then, the 'haves', the 1 per cent, drove motor cars, which, like their clothing, were bespoke. Mother knew only the name of the Head Gardener, because there were too many other gardeners and, anyway, no instructions were to be given without being passed first through Mr Edwards. He wore a three-piece suit with a gold watch chain across his prosperous paunch. The others, the 'have nots', still walked to the pump down the street for water and hoarded coal to warm the house a little on Christmas Eve – coal in your stocking was a blessing, not a scold in those days. This 99 per cent who produced everything, died in wars 'for their country' and served the gentry hand and foot. Only, twenty years later, there were no more servants and everyone bought what they could afford and find.

There certainly remained anomalies, such as the barber whom Father occasionally visited in London. I remember the place after the war, with its dark wood-framed bevelled mirrors and great high, stuffed leather armchairs around which glided the Gentleman Barbers, armed with hand clippers and scissors, long razors which they stropped on leather – the same genteel old men who had regularly trimmed the beard of King George V. They were masters of conversation, no doubt researching the interests of the morrow's client the night before – sport was not the dominant subject as it is today, but gentle mention of Politics, Art,

Literature and (for Father) even Sailing! Or Jacksons of Piccadilly, where you could still see an immaculate 'Gentleman's Gentleman' tasting a little aged stilton, only to declare that "His Lordship would not approve, it's under-ripe, you see".

In general, while still hugely divided, there had been a giant leap towards egalitarianism. When working on his second novel, Father had consulted a Chinese laundryman (who spoke enough English) on details of local colour from his past. He was researching his next book (which came out in 1938) and when the man mentioned that he would like to open his own laundry, instead of working for someone else, Father gave him five pounds and asked him to bill him when he had used up his credit. He posted his dirty dress shirts to London and they came back immaculately starched and ironed – and he was never asked for another penny – those five pounds had been seed capital that started a small Chinese laundry empire! Not that Father wore dress shirts by the time I was around in North Wales – well, perhaps once a year. He wore modern nylon shirts that he washed himself and hung to dry in the bathroom. Unlike his old friend Dylan Thomas, he had several shirts, whereas Dylan only bought one for his first lecture tour in the States – he said he tried to wash it every night, but since it was never dry in the morning, he always put it on wet next day. Much like the vicar who announced that his dog collar was made of plastic, so he could "lick it clean in the morning and it was ready to wear!"

Sixty years on, I found the car again, when my brother sent me an e-mail with an attachment: a couple of black-and-white snapshots of it at its very worst, slumped by a stone wall in a small field belonging to our friend Hamish, high up in the Welsh mountains. Pieces of body were hanging down to the ground or removed and loaded onto the seats. Then there were glossy colour photographs of it immaculately restored, with its original licence plate: KU631, outside an expensive suburban brick house somewhere in England, its distinctive body changed beyond recognition. The gracefully long, sweeping wings – so modern for a car built in 1922 – had been replaced by small individual mudguards. The only access door was on the passenger side because the handbrake was exterior. Even the gear stick was on the outside of the driver, though inside the car. This left more room for the passenger and an easier slide-through for the driver when getting in. I suppose it also left no excuse for groping the skirts of attractive young flappers while changing gears. His was the 113th Bentley to leave the workshop, the original body built by a private coachbuilder – as was the custom in those days.

Just as Fords came "in every colour as long as it's black" and all early Bugattis came in bright blue, so all Bentleys were British Racing Green, a green so dark as to be almost black. It had last changed hands for £75,000. I believe Father had bought it second-hand in 1928 for the phenomenally high price of £2,000 (say, £100,000 today). He was doing well in those days.

II

THE FIRST WINTERS

Was that really my very first memory: when I was six? Or was it, more likely, when I was sitting on my wooden lorry, called Borry, pushing it up the incline of flagstones in a huge kitchen at the age of three? After the Second World War, there were no metal toys to buy, no Dinky or Tonka Toys, just what local artisans could make from bits of wood and nails and wire. That was how Borry was created.

The floor of that kitchen seemed to stretch and slope as far as the eye could see. There was a great, hot coal stove to cook on that kept the whole room cosy. I wonder how we had any coal, in that post-war time of rationing and penury – when women in the cities were queuing up for their coal rations with prams in which to take it home. Yet we seemed to have coal and no doubt that was why I was playing there when it happened. The winter of '46/'47 was particularly cold in Cumberland, just south of the Scottish/English border. We stayed there, at Lyulph's Tower (which belonged to Hubert Howard, one of Mother's first cousins), for a winter because our house in North Wales was still impractical for winter living. For a start, our new home had no legal access (save by sea) and it was hard work bringing coal two miles across the estuary by boat at high tide. Besides, petrol was still rationed and Father could not get petrol coupons for his outboard motor, so he had to use some of the precious supply intended for the Jeep.

So it was that we spent those two winters in different houses in Cumberland (also known as the Lake District). They belonged to one or another of Mother's numerous cousins: Howards, the Catholic side of the family. Some of their ancestors had lost their heads rather than renounce their faith during the Reformation of the sixteenth century. The Doyen of that family was John, first Duke of Norfolk (1430-85)... the present Duke is so far removed from my family as to be beyond my sight. Lyulph's Tower had been built as a hunting lodge almost a hundred years before, in Victorian times, in a bizarre style of 'Gothic Castle', a nineteenth-century version of some 1940s Beverly Hills folly. It had a vast kitchen and dining hall in which to prepare and enjoy the spoils of the hunt. Its Gothic style left complicated joints in the roof where great weights of snow accumulated. Leaks occurred where the lead flashing had failed. The leaks wet the heavy plaster ceilings below, until...

Bang! – there was a terrific crash as a huge piece of thick ceiling plaster plummeted to the floor, throwing up a fountain of dust about it. I remember watching, fascinated by the cloud of dust that rose, spread like a mushroom, and then slowly fell back to the floor. The chunks of plaster had whiskers of horsehair (added to the plaster to give it greater structural strength) protruding from its sides, where it had broken off and landed – just where I had been on my lorry only a few moments before. That startled me and no doubt, startled Mother even more.

That time in the Lake District, I first heard the word '*terrific*' and sensed the exhilaration of a forceful, enthusiastic speaker. I was sitting between two adults in the huge, leather front seat of a Ford Motorcar (no such thing as seat belts then), climbing the driveway of Lyulph's Tower, that Gothic Hunting Lodge. The car smelled of musty wood, leather and hot oil, that nostalgic odour of old motors which still grabs at my senses as evocatively as certain perfumes. The driver was a commanding old lady and she exploded the word '*terrific*' with such vehemence that it has stayed in heavy italics with me to this day. It remains associated with the simple replica of an aeroplane that decorated the hoods of those big old Ford Pilots. It gave me visions of planes taking flight – the soaring force, the escape, the flight... all contained in that single word '*terrific!*' At that age I did not wonder where the precious petrol to run this big car came from, but it certainly was strictly rationed at the time.

I wonder now if that determined lady was our Great Aunt 'Tiger', who terrified the whole county with her driving – a style not so dissimilar to that of Mother. They both drove by touch rather than by sight, punctuating monologues by forcefully changing gears – usually at the wrong moment for the car. Tiger had knocked down a 'pillar box' or mailbox at the end of her driveway. Pillar boxes were of heavy cast iron, set deep into the ground and painted bright red (how could you possibly miss them?) They were decorated with the Royal Coat-of-Arms and 'G.R.VI' for 'George Rex Sixth'. The Royal Mail and its collection boxes were the property of the Crown and their abuse a serious offence. Nevertheless, when Great Aunt Tiger was summoned to the magistrate's court, she stormed in with all guns blazing, upbraiding the sixty-year-old magistrate with: "Now listen to me, young man, that pillar box was placed in a most dangerous position. Someone was bound to run into it sooner or later. It must be moved to a safer place!" It was moved and Great Aunt Tiger continued to terrify the neighbourhood by driving around for many years to come.

While the War was in its final, desperate death-throes – successful at last thanks to Roosevelt's skilful manipulation of American opinion, I had already managed to half cripple my left hand by holding onto the heating bar of an electric heater. It was off at the time, but incorrectly wired, so that even when turned off, electricity still flowed when given the 'ground' of a crawling infant. I was too young to have any memories of this, but I was later told that my youngest sister, three years my senior, was so terrified by my blackened hand that she screamed until Mother came and picked her up – ignoring, for the time being, the source of her horror: the hand! Well, that falling ceiling missed me too. How many lives does one have? At least in North Wales there would be no danger of electrocution – we had a twelve-volt windmill charging four tractor batteries. They were usually so worn out that the light came up and died down again on the whim of the wind as it freshened and failed – much as a sailing boat drifts to a standstill in a calm, then lists to the wind and leaps forward again. No, there was no danger of electrocution here!

Ten years later, my middle finger was still so bent from the burn that it threatened to grow into my palm. I was sent to a hospital for plastic surgery. The hospital had been built during the Second World War to patch up disfigured fighter pilots. It still looked like an army barracks but now it treated hare-lips and obtrusive ears in children, besides casualties of fires and accidents amongst adults. In three weeks the surgeons did miracles and the finger is as good as new.

Nor could I escape electrocution forever: in the sixties I was installing a kinetic art show in a gallery on the Boulevard St Germain, in Paris. Noon came just as I was in the middle of some complex wiring, but when the six artists setting up their own works called me to lunch, I dropped everything in midstream and we all went round the corner to a neighbourhood bistro for a well-lubricated lunch and much enthusiastic discussion. We were just behind Les Deux Magots, hangout and workplace of Hemingway, Sartre and Camus – but it was too busy and expensive for us proletarian workers. Upon our return an hour later, what I had been doing had escaped me and I had forgotten what I should do next. I decided simply to pick up where I had left off and hope it would all come back to me. The metal-handled wire cutters were still there on the floor where I had left them, right next to the wire which I was about to cut. The bang threw me right across the room. I could see the wire was still plugged in – the outlet smoking ominously. My wire cutters were perfectly melted to use as wire strippers with two small rounds melted in the cutting edges. Could that have been why I moved to America, where the voltage is 110 instead of 220?

The next year, in this peripatetic, half-homeless life, we spent the winter in a real medieval castle called Naworth, also part of the Howard fiefdom in Cumberland. It had been converted into four living units, each with a corner tower and one long, narrow, habitable wall of rooms. Father wrote in the great gallery, a room perhaps a hundred feet long, lined with portraits of ancestors – ideal for pacing to and fro as he cogitated.

Alas I was too young to participate in a battle, organized by my older siblings. The children of the castle defended it against an onslaught of neighbouring friends and cousins. They used paper bags full of flour and the fire hoses and stirrup pumps intended for serious defence of the castle in a conflagration. Everyone finished up looking like papier-mâché puppets. The courtyard was partially flooded from the fire hoses and in the night it froze. Next day I went sliding on the ice and Mother broke her coccyx, falling on some outdoor stone steps. She had to sit painfully on a doughnut-shaped cushion for many weeks thereafter.

I do not know if we were really hungry in those days (as one of my sisters tells me), but I do remember where Mother had hidden the precious, rationed ingredients to make a Christmas pudding. There were raisins, sultanas and lots of sugar. I had never before seen such sweet bounty and soon made myself thoroughly sick out loud (as Mother too graph-ically termed the act of vomiting!) I am sure I was severely punished and no one, myself included, was happy with the greatly diminished size of the pudding. However green I looked after being sick out loud, it did not stop me from going to Mother one day and saying: "Owain's pale and weakly, Doctor says he needs more choccy." Disgusting child that I was...

On Christmas Day, I was in bed with my youngest sister. We were exploring our stockings – what could be more wonderful for two very young children to find in their Christmas stockings than a whole fresh honeycomb from a neighbour's hives? We scooped out the honey with our fingers until they went right through the wax on the other side and honey flowed stickily everywhere. I particularly remember how delightful it felt between my toes... until some grown-up came with harsh words and clean sheets.

That winter, I often played with a boy of my age and eventually caught whooping cough from him. His father owned a four-seated air taxi. At the time, the favoured cure for whooping cough was to fly in an unpressurised plane to 5 or 7,000 metres... so, from whom better to catch the wretched bug than the son of the owner of an air taxi? I loved the flight, soaring over the rolling lush green hills and dark, almost black tarns or inland meres of the Lake District and buzzing Naworth Castle until people came outside and waved... but I came back still whooping, while my friend shook it off.

There was a biochemist friend of my Parents, who had inherited some vast expanse of highland with its peat bogs. There was an old tradition of cutting blocks of peat and drying them for sale as a heating fuel. I remember the miles of narrow-gauge railway tracks across the moors with small wagons pushed by men to bring in the harvested peat blocks. This friend decided to set up a factory to make other products from the peat. After each product was produced, there was always a by-product left over which he made into something else until finally there was a colourless, odourless, slightly viscous material with high heat-retaining properties – he sold it to an ice cream factory as an additive filler. That was the part I remember so vividly, though it would be some years before I actually tasted this mythological treat known as ice cream.

Soon after the whooping cough interlude, Mother and I

flew down to North Wales with our friend the air taxi man. I remember clearly how we circled low over Snowdonia. The day was sunny and clear; each rock and each path stood out vividly below. The grass was emerald green, the lakes the deepest blue and the craggy rocks in greys and blacks. There were many tiny walkers and climbers below, wearing bright clothing, hiking up the easier paths. The exhilaration of flying over this scene was god-like. I caught another bug up there in that tiny plane: from then on, I wanted to know those rocks and crags and precipices intimately. I wanted to break them as one breaks a wild stallion. I wanted to learn to conquer them by scaling their rugged heights and scrambling over them.

Almost twenty years later (as a young man) one Easter day in Paris, I flew once more over those brilliantly clear mountains, crags and lakes – this time without a plane, just on the power of Beethoven's Fifth Symphony which entered my eyes as a full-spectrum rainbow and left through my outstretched arms, from under my fingernails. The rainbow flowed through me and supported my flight as I turned left and right, sweeping up like a raven on the updraft, then gliding down into the valleys. Later that day we ran through the courtyards of the Louvre and saw the significance of architecture as it defines the open space within it, just as much as it exists in the form of walls, floors and windows. For the first time, I saw and appreciated *empty* space as architecture. Now I came to understand that you can construct empty space as an edifice by defining that space with walls.

Suddenly, the bouncing of the aircraft on the multiple up and downdrafts over the mountains took its toll. The pilot quickly handed me a paper airsickness bag. Once used, he slid open the cockpit canopy and tossed it out... I had a dreadful image of the bag landing squarely on the unsuspecting head of a passing, sweating hiker... but was assured that it would disintegrate on the way down. Anyway, when those hills did indeed become my playground and I hiked for days and nights on end, I never feared being crowned with a vomit-laden paper bag. For one thing, it's very tricky flying in these mountains, with such violent thermals and I have no recollection of ever seeing light aircraft flying low over those mountains. Many a mountain rescue helicopter has crashed. Endangering oneself is one thing, but doing so endangers many others.

We flew on south towards our house on its estuary and located a field a mile or two away, where the locals said a small plane had landed during the War. It turned out to be surrounded on all four sides by power lines, besides having high banks underneath with hedges growing on them. The surprised pilot said it was quite impossible to land there. Even if he could fly under the wires and over the banks and hedges, he could never take off again. We flew on and tried the beach of the estuary in front of our house. We must have radio-telephoned Father, because he was already on the beach with our American Army Jeep, waiting for us.

The pilot thought he could land where there were 'car tracks' on the sand, but one very tentative touch-and-go threatened to flip the plane over in a somersault and he was not prepared to try again... Father in his Jeep had been driving on soft sand which was totally unsuitable for landing. By this time, most of the anti-aircraft poles (of which, more later) had been removed, but the sand remained stubbornly deep and soft.

We flew west, towards the open sea and there, by the salt marshes where I would later spend happy hours trying to shoot wild duck, we found an unobstructed field. Hoping that there were no rabbit holes to catch our wheels, we landed with some wrenching bangs, bumps and bounces. That was where Father finally chased us down. Later, we learned that the famous field where we had first tried to land had killed the pilot and crew of the only aircraft to land there – a fatal crash-landing due to engine trouble! A small detail that was missing in local lore which might well have made all the difference in the recommendation...

III

HOME

On the edge of a great tidal estuary, twice daily trans-formed from sea to sand to sea again, sits a simple square white house. It was to become our long-term home over the next thirty years. The tides from the estuary come in from the Irish Sea, which is warmed by the Gulf Stream from the Caribbean. It sweeps all the way up the east coast of the United States, then across the North Atlantic, before embracing the coasts of Brittany, the Scilly Isles and up between Wales and Ireland. Yet it remains a current warm enough to temper these latitudes. At sea level, a freeze is exceptional; a few hundred feet up and away from the sea, it's a very different story. The opposite shore is a rocky promontory (dividing twin estuaries) that had belonged to a wealthy amateur botanist in the nineteenth century. He had brought back specimens of rhododendron from Nepal, bamboo from China and redwood from California and had planted a lush forest garden on the promontory, to this day called the Gwyllt (or 'Wilderness'). His large house, with its tall, barley-sugar chimneys, nestles down on the edge of the tidal estuary, constantly changing from sand to sea or sand and sea. The property was bought by the celebrated architect and environmentalist, Clough Williams-Ellis in the mid-1920s and converted into an eccentric hotel, his 'Experiment in Sympathetic Development': Portmeirion. From our house, a mile away, it looked like a brightly coloured Italianate village in the distance. He denied being influenced by Portofino (which he must have known, even then, but the parallel becomes more evident further on in this story). As a very young child I had precociously declared that Portmeirion had been built during the '*Early Ice Cream Age*'... what did I know of ice cream at the time? The hotel remained a magical mélange of architectural styles, a mirage in my mind. As for the frozen dessert, I had to wait for refrigeration and the end of sugar rationing... for Britain maintained food rationing until 1954 largely because of the cost of maintaining its armaments (three full Naval fleets and one-hundred-and-twenty RAF squadrons worldwide).

The estuary is a mile across and some days, when the sun shines, the shadows of clouds chase each other across the brilliantly-lit expanses of sand and water, bringing a rapidly-changing light, like a fast-forward film of clouds. Ever changing from grey to bright light – moody as Mother. It was true that Father could also explode like a thunder-clap when disturbed by children's games. He had a huge voice and large presence. His anger was an avalanche or violent squall, driving us noise-makers into submissive silence and seclusion. Some child once remarked that: "Daddy's thundering again."

The situation of the house was remote and wild beyond what one might imagine of Britain – and indeed remains largely unspoilt to this day. True, we could see the hotel a mile away across the estuary and a few other houses appeared as tiny dots still further off. On the far side of the twin estuary stood the small, silted-up harbour town of Porthmadog, but that is two miles away. On a very still night, one might hear the train a mile and a half away, but otherwise there were no sounds of civilization, no cars, or trucks, or buses. Our neighbours on either side were several hundred yards away. To the east was old Mr Edwards (the farmer) who had no motor, save his son's old lorry for the hay harvest. To the west stood the house of old Mrs Thomas who must have had some money because she drove a little old Ford from the 1930s, but with petrol rationing, she used it only once every two weeks. Since none of us had electricity, motor mowers, chain saws or today's other noisy contraptions, the only noise was the sound of the seagulls, the wind and perhaps the waves at high tide. In the isolated silence, we could hear the blood pressure pounding in our ears – a rhythmic reminder that we were alive, but certainly no proof that anyone else in the whole wide world was also alive...

Then the clouds would pour rain here and there on the scene, while all the rest remained in bright sunlight. Much of the time, the mountains to the north were shrouded from view by thick cloud and sometimes, even the mile-away coast opposite disappeared completely and rain would pour down for many days on end. We spent day after day reading, until our Parents went out. Then, in holiday times, when some of my siblings were around, we could burst out with our raucous indoor games.

Behind this little oasis of lush gardens and colour on the opposite shore, rise the sharp peaks of the Snowdonia range, craggy summits soaring from treeless slopes, snow-clad during the winter months, an ever-changing view of spectacular depth. Squalls of grey rain clouds would veil the brilliance of blue sky. The mountains themselves turned from pale blue in the misty light to deep blue in clearer light or were veiled completely, those sharp crags far away, inaccessible as a Romantic painting of the eighteenth or nineteenth century, frameless as the open sky. They were intangible in their distance. The very concept of access, the idea of walking their slopes, climbing the crags seemed quite inconceivable – yet in fact is so very real. At times, there was a brooding calm but again later, it could be fierce and tempestuous, ferocious, magical. It was a constantly shifting scene. This is no theatre backdrop, but natural scenery. This is the view from our family home. Sixty years later, it is a view that still takes my breath away when I get out to open the farm gate at the top of the hill behind the house and look down over the vast panorama when I visit it again, (after an overnight flight from New York to Manchester). This is the view that I have left behind. It belongs to another life, a could-have-been life that I do not, for a moment, regret not having pursued.

This white house was built in 1911 to serve as a base for a headmaster (John Chambers) and his family, while his pupils camped in a field next door. An additional wing was added after the First World War. It was never intended as a year-round residence, so our eight-bedroom home was very simple, even utilitarian – but the situation spectacular. Behind it rose a small hill, the 'Ynys' or Island – for it was a tidal island until the end of the nineteenth century and going back seven hundred years (when Harlech Castle was built) it was a full-time island with access only by boat or perhaps at low tide over the sands.

In those early days, Arthur Koestler (the intensely *engagé* Hungarian writer) and his wife Cynthia had come to dinner with us in Wales, despite the difficult access to our house. Afterwards, Father escorted them the half mile, in the pitch-black night, along the sea grass that was carved by deep gullies where the tide ran out and edged the estuary, to where the old driveway was washed out and came to an end, where their car was parked. The tide had risen, leading Koestler to remark that he was almost drowned on the way back. "Nonsense," said Father afterwards, "he never stopped talking for a second, I would have known at once if he was drowning, there would have been a moment's peace!"

The estuary used to be forked, the northern part having been dammed in 1811 to create arable land on that reclaimed branch. The southern fork, where our house stands, is still tidal: twice a day, the seven by one mile estuary is transformed from sand with a few streams in it, to being completely full of water. At spring tides there can be a vertical rise and fall of up to 11.5 metres. Tides governed whole sectors of our lives and respect for the lethal currents was in our veins. To this day, tourists drown where we children played. For one thing, the warning signs are usually illegible and, even when they are decipherable, often only in Welsh. At home, the tide table always hung on a string in the 'telephone room', to be consulted before planning a dinner, accepting an invitation or making any other daily plans, whether building sand castles, setting and cleaning the nets, baiting the night-lines, collecting the fish, going sailing, riding or shooting.

Our family was broadly divided into two camps: sailors and horse people. Father headed the first, though he also rode well enough to have gone pig-sticking for wild boar in Morocco, where a fall during the chase could be fatal. The second camp was under Mother's tutelage, though she too could row a dinghy with the best in an emergency. My brother (the eldest of the family) and my eldest sister were sailors, while the next two sisters, horsewomen. As we were of an uneven number, I fell between the two camps, though it was impractical to be a member of both sides. The amount of upkeep demanded by old clinker-built wooden boats on one side, and ponies and horses on the other, made adherence to both at once just too much work. There are not enough hours of light in the day. We could all do both, but we had our preferences and priorities.

I wanted to be a sailor (and have been all my life) but my horse-riding sisters could not resist the urge to use me as a jockey in one-mile pony races. I was young enough to be in a special class and light enough to race the smallest pony. Apparently, I had cold feet at the last moment before my first race at the age of seven, and had to be given Dutch courage in the form of hard cider, which was more alcoholic than beer. After a large glass of that, I forgot my fear, raced as if the devil was on my back, missed the last post in a haze of alcohol and started to retire – only to be told that everyone else had already missed several posts. I turned back into the race and just won it anyway. My sisters had another red rosette to hang in the tack room!

There were occasional squabbles between the two factions. Had the boat people stolen the grain scoop to use as a bailer? Had the horse people stolen a line to tether a horse? I never bonded with horses and later experiences have done nothing to elevate things equine in my estimation. I rented a knock-kneed skeleton of a horse in the Taurus mountains of southern Turkey, only to have it fall off the path we were on and roll down the mountain with me and my camera underneath. The camera fared even worse than I. In fact, nowadays, I think: "*the only animals more stupid than horses are the ones that sit on top of them.*"

Both hobbies involved escape in several forms. Horses and boats themselves escape and have to be brought home. Such moments required an 'all-hands-on-deck' response, so the horse people joined in rescuing boats and vice versa. Besides, sailors and horsemen alike revel in the joys of solitude and evasion, whether sailing away for a few miles on a high tide, or riding along the vast open sands, or up into the wild mountains. Cousins and friends came to stay and frequently needed rescuing, either from a cantering pony as they called out: "Where are the brakes?" or a boat they had taken downstream on an ebbing tide. Father showed them no compassion or sympathy. He would just say, peremptorily: "You'll have go back and get it on the next tide," even though that might well have been at midnight or later. One of us would have to go with them to help them retrieve the boat or the pony, west, down the estuary to the sand bar before the open sea or east, up the estuary to a tidal island called Ynys Gifftan.

On that island, there was a tiny farmhouse where a tenant farmer and his wife tried to make a living by grazing sheep and cattle on the salt flats, where the domesticated animals lived a 'turf war' on the salt grass with the Canada geese. Cows would often drink the rainwater out of our boats at low tide, the only trouble being that they would try to climb into them, and sharp hooves on the floor of a wooden dinghy on dry land can cause a great deal of damage – so we would chase them off. The farmer had a small horse and cart for going to and fro at low tide. One day, he and his wife could no longer bear the isolation (like us, they were without electricity but did not even have a telephone) so they decided to move to Chicago. They held a sale and sold everything they owned. A short time later, they returned, saying that: "they would rather cross the estuary at night on a rising spring tide, than traverse the smallest street in Chicago." News went around that they were back and, knowing that they were flat broke, everyone brought back what they had bought at the sale. No one asked for their money back, everyone knew they had none left. Everyone, that is, except Father, who had bought a china bowl, which had only lasted a week in its new home before being broken, to our shame. In the end, they only moved off the island to the cemetery and the adventure of Chicago lived on (as a somewhat embarrassing attempt at escape) in their own minds.

IV

THE HOUSE

The outside of the house is pebble-dash, painted with whitewash. We painted it ourselves every few years, adding a touch of blue or pink dye to the white – unnoticeable in sunlight, but coming through in the rain – a joyful relief when everything was grey and sodden. One wing might glow in the rain the palest shade of blue, another just hardly pink. The roof was of fine local slate, so dark it was black when wet.

As a teenager in the late fifties, I had wire brushed the rust from the cast-iron gutters and was painting them with an extension ladder leaning on the gutters. Going up and down two high storeys on the ladder was a bore, so I tried bouncing the ladder over so that I could paint the small patch where the ladder had been. It bounced nicely and landed on wet paint and *swoosh!* away it went! Sailors are half monkey, so clinging to the sturdy cast-iron gutter, I caught the ladder with my toes and managed to haul it back up and out onto the gutter again. A close shave! Saved by the great strength of those gutters (today's aluminium or plastic would never have held me – but then, neither would they need scraping and painting!)

When we first arrived at the house in 1946, the large sash windows were criss-crossed with heavy black tape, a precaution in the event of enemy bombing during the War that was only just over. This gave the vivid impression of being imprisoned behind thick steel bars. It was quickly removed, but their image still haunts me. Prison. Being imprisoned. Behind bars. Incarcerated.

Indeed when we arrived, the estuary was still thickly forested with naked trees: half telegraph poles planted deep in the sand, creosoted to stop rot, and connected to each other by heavy fencing wire. This was to stop enemy aircraft from landing in the estuary or landing craft coming in from the sea. Soon enough, most of the poles were dug up, scavenged for more constructive peacetime uses. A few poles remained for some years and we used them for navigation. Sometimes, when suitably located, they even served as one of the stakes for Father's fishing nets.

There was really nothing worth bombing nearby, except of course the Roman Camp. On British Ordnance Survey maps, historic sites are marked in gothic font. When the German army was planning targets, they found such a site marked Military Camp (not even Roman Military Camp) and sent out a very small mission to bomb it. The greatest damage (it was high up on the hills, far from any modern dwelling) was to a mound that turned out to be a huge pile of oyster shells. The Romans loved their oysters. Oysters have since disappeared from this part of the coast and have only recently been re-introduced. Either the climate has changed enough for them to have gone, or two thousand years ago, the Romans had eaten every last one! I discount theories that they could have been brought all the way from the South coast of England on mules... without ice? Even bringing them from the Welsh coast to their hilltop fort without spoilage must have been quite a feat. The stupid mistake by the Boche command delighted us, the exhausted, impoverished victors.

Within, the house had bare floors – the institutional brown linoleum having been mostly torn up by my Parents, exposing the bare pine planking beneath. The exception was Father's study. The frequent rain meant that mud and sand were perpetually tracked inside, so carpets would have been impractical. The scene was set as you entered the front door: a large square hall with the floor tiled in black and white squares set on the diagonal. On one side stood a full-sized rocking horse that had seen the abuse of many generations. On the other sat an iron chest, said to have been captured in the Armada. It had a remarkably complex lock that took up the entire lid, though the key was missing. In front of the entrance was a round marble mosaic table from Italy. On the walls hung three de Chirico paintings, setting a truly surrealist scene.

On either side of the front door, in niches backed with glass to the outdoors, were two white marble busts: a beautiful and fashionable lady in *décolleté* and a handsome young man with classical features and no shirt. The front door was never locked. There was no key until finally our insurance company told my Parents that they could not claim theft of any of their valuable paintings, without a 'breaking and entering'. Father took off the lock and brought it to the locksmith to have a key made. A few months later, they were planning a trip to the Mediterranean and Father went in search of the locksmith. He was told that the man was at a hill farm fitting a lock. Finally Father found the locksmith and he was in fact just fitting our lock to the farm door. When Father protested, he said: "Well I made up a key and then I couldn't remember whose lock it was, so it just sat around the workshop until I needed a lock for someone." There was no argument and Father finally brought back the lock, this time with a key!

We never had newspapers in the house – Father listened to the BBC news on a succession of bulky 'portable' radios with valves and two large, heavy batteries. I do, however, remember one newspaper, laid out carefully on the round mosaic table: it was heavily edged in black and it bore the single headline: 'His Royal Highness King George VI died last night' – which would date it as: February 7, 1952 (when I was eight). Mother had a lifelong admiration for the Royal Family (her youngest sister was lady-in-waiting to Queen Elizabeth for almost fifty years). I wonder why I was not at my new weekly boarding school in London. There was no knowing what special arrangements my Parents might have made due to their eccentric lives, their travels – or perhaps I was at home sick at the time. At all events, the family's plans were in continual flux, ever changing, like the weather, with moods and circumstances, but never as foreseeable as the tides which keep strictly to their moon cycle.

Giving onto the front hall to the left were two rooms with spectacular views across the estuary to the barren, sharp, rocky mountains of Snowdonia beyond. One was Mother's painting study, its bare pine floor painted sky blue, stacks of paintings leaning against every wall. A large 1930s modernist desk of pale wood stood to one side.

The other room was Father's inner-sanctum: lined floor to ceiling with books, carpeted from wall to wall, Moroccan rugs as well, heavy Empire furniture, heavy velvet curtains, the air thick with pipe smoke. Behind the door, rested two or three 12-bore shotguns, a Winchester .22 (with silencer and telescopic sights), two Moroccan flint-lock muskets, a rapier and a sabre. On the mantle piece were a couple of Moroccan daggers with 30cm blades – the kind of useful ornament carried by most robed gentlemen there. Indeed, a few years later, when I was leaving for points East, I showed Father the sheath knife I wanted to take. He at once discouraged me (and I followed his advice) saying: "they carry and use knives all their lives, a man attacked will wrest your knife from you with ease and then will know how to use it. Go off without arms, because even if you think they will protect you, they will be turned against you."

There was also a stuffed baby crocodile – a memorial to the two baby crocs he tried to bring away from Jamaica in the washbasin of his cabin. Ratted on by his steward, the captain had them thrown overboard – they would have needed a whole bathtub each by the time they reached England, and then what? First alligators in the New York sewage system, now crocodiles loose on the hills of Snowdonia?

Piles of typescripts covered every horizontal surface, from a beautifully polished round table, to a well-worn leather button couch, his huge desk and even the floor. Unless Father was out working on his fishing nets or in the kitchen garden, that front entrance hall was totally forbidden to us children during the day lest we disturb his train of thought, in the muffled cocoon of his study. Even the noise of Canada geese on the salt sea grass or the sound of the black Labrador, breathing rhythmically in her sleep by the fire, was too much of an interruption for him. The breathing upset his literary stride that moved to a different drummer. The honking just startled him out of his absorbed reverie. We could come in by the back door to the pantry and from there to the kitchen or up the back stairs to our rooms. Besides, even though there was a kind of 'lock' at the front door, with a small space between the actual front door and an interior door, opening them both at once during a south-westerly gale erased any attempt at warming the house.

There were the front stairs that led upstairs in two flights. On the landing windowsill was an assemblage of stuffed Caribbean birds and another of white corals – both under huge, fragile glass domes. At the top, there was a landing where a couple of paintings by Winifred Nicholson, wife of the famous painter Ben Nicholson, whose brother, architect Christopher Nicholson had designed the dining room table which I have in New York to this day. The Nicholson family were old friends of my Parents, but we did not have any of Ben's work – it was already too geometric for their tastes. Nancy, his sister, was married to Robert Graves. There were also paintings by Kate Nicholson, daughter of Winifred.

To the right was the kitchen door. This was always the warmest room in the house, thanks to an Aga stove and hot water boiler, both coke burning. Next, came the door to the telephone room with its single window, with a huge gold-brown velvet curtain, so long it trailed on the floor, and a windowsill upon which sat the telephone. Already, the telephone no longer had a crank – but then, it didn't have a dial either. You simply picked up the receiver and eventually the operator (could it really always have been the same woman?) would reply. You might say: "Good morning, may I speak to Williams Taxi?" and the reply might be: "Well now, Gwylim just took Mrs. Jones the bacon all the way to Bangor. Got a lump, she says. Hurting something terrible. Doctor sent her to the hospital indeed. Mind you, he should be back this evening. Kind man, Gwylim, never a hard word. Expensive, they say…" Did anyone ever just hang up on her and decide to walk or hitch-hike rather than bother to call a friend, or try to reach the one and only taxi? In winter, Mother would wind the velvet curtain around her, to keep warm. It looked like a cocoon, with a telephone cord emerging from its depths.

The telephone was not a familiar contraption to many people in Wales at the time. Several times Father called the farmhouse at the top of the hill, when he was away, to ask if they would turn on our water and leave it running, because a freeze was expected and the water line would freeze up. Once, the telephone rang for a long time and the operator did not pick up, until finally a frightened voice said: "It's only the mother of Grace" and hung up – 'Grace' was the operator. Another time, he reached the operator and asked for the neighbouring farm, where a different, confused voice answered: "There's nobody here!"

Beyond the telephone room came the living/dining room with its scrubbed pine floor and scrubbed twelve-foot sycamore table. It had been made for my Parents' wedding in 1932, of unseasoned wood but designed to shrink symmetrically. Raw, unbleached linen-covered couches surrounded the fireplace and a stuffed gannet sat on its base on a side table. On the wall above the bird, hung a brilliantly gay, great Raoul Dufy Mediterranean seascape of a sailing regatta off Cannes, one of his best, I believe. On another wall there was a large gloomy, foreboding North Sea storm scene by the naïve fisherman-painter Crask. A gaily-coloured Matisse-like portrait of a Moroccan servant by Edward Wolfe hung over the fireplace and a moody portrait of Mother by Augustus John (finished and signed) hung to the left of the fireplace. Another Augustus John, unsigned and unfinished, of Father as a young man, hung at the far end of the long dining table.

When Mother's portrait was brought in to hang, I asked who "that horrid, cross lady is." Little did I know then, the myth that runs amongst many Augustus John admirers: that, while he was often not satisfied with portraits of men and so left them unfinished and unsigned (I know of three of my own Father), those women whose portraits he had finished and signed he had also bedded. But then, he was a well-known 'ladies' man' and often claimed conquests that may never have gone any further than his own head! At all events, none of us looked in the least like him… Indeed, I was later shown a dedication by the painter to Father, in pale pencil on the face of the painting. Surely he would not have had the gall to give him the portrait after cuckolding him? No doubt I am only too eager to ascribe a lively sex life to Mother, since she later told me that I was "a delightful surprise" after Father (at forty-two) lost all interest.

The comfortable, somewhat broken-down couches were a mine of treasures: under the cushions there was frequently some spare change which had escaped from people's pockets, but also, Mother sometimes hid the sewing or darning she was doing at the moment someone paid a visit. Pins and needles were normal fare and her long cutting shears could also be hidden under the cushions… making casual, blind exploration full of pitfalls – it was wiser to wait for some privacy, then raise the cushions and look. Just delving with unseeing hands could be a painful experience! Between the couches and the fireplace lay a very threadbare lion's skin with its stuffed head rearing up in a perpetual snarl.

Father told the story of a little girl (no doubt a grandmother by now) who was staying with us and came down early to breakfast. He discovered her, terrified by the snarling lion's head and standing on a chair, clutching her skirt around her knees like a Victorian Miss who has espied a mouse in the corner! Mother responded by telling how, as a child staying with a great-uncle, her governess would bring the children down for breakfast in the breakfast room, but she herself would always make a quick detour, just to check to see if the rhinoceros, whose head was thrust right through the wall into the dining room, had managed to come in any further during the night!

Every room in the house, even the telephone room and the entrance hall, had its own little fireplace grate, for burning coal. Most were never used. The electrical grid had not reached even the hamlet a mile away, on the other side of the hill, so electricity simply could not be obtained. Father had wired the house himself, with the aid of an electrician. It was a 12-volt system charged by a windmill that was tethered to one corner of the house, making that bedroom shake during heavy windstorms. The light was insufficient to read by. The light bulbs used were the size of ping pong balls and were unobtainable during post-war rationing. Visitors coming from London might ask what they could bring with them, some "Stilton cheese or coffee perhaps?" Instead Father would ask them to ride a double-decker bus and steal some bulbs from the upper deck when the conductor was not looking. We received quite a few such gifts from distinguished citizens turned kleptomaniacs, just for us.

I was sleeping in the windmill-corner bedroom – it had been my brother's, but by then he was almost never at home – when there was a surprise in the morning. I looked out of the window at the line of accessory buildings that housed the stable, tool room, an outside toilet and the coal room. The roof of the coal room was gone. In my sleep-befuddled state, I thought that a stork had come to nest on its slate roof, proved too heavy and it had collapsed! I hated that coal room.

I was frequently sent out with a cylindrical coalscuttle to get fuel at night. It was always pitch dark and I imagined that, camouflaged by the noise I had to make, scooping up coal (for the open fires), or coke (smokeless, for the kitchen stove and boiler), anything or anyone could jump on me from behind, perhaps cleave me in half with a hatchet. That was always my greatest fear, far more than scaling cliffs or setting out for long hikes alone. As it turned out, no stork was involved: someone had put hot coal ashes in there, which had caught afire again, set off the coal and the roof beams had burned. The slates, which had fallen to the ground, were mostly intact and once the wooden frame had been replaced, were re-hung in place.

Another morning, Father awakened me, dressed as usual, barefoot, with his grey flannel trousers rolled up to the knee and a threadbare tweed jacket over an old cable-knit sweater full of holes. He smelled of pipe smoke, seaweed and fish. His eyes twinkled above his greying beard as he ceremoniously plunged his hand deep inside an inner pocket of his jacket and produced a large, torpedo-shaped sea-bass (or branzino). Not many of them came up our estuary and when we caught one, it was a most welcome alternative to plaice. The idea of putting his day's catch in his jacket pockets was no more eccentric than having a rocking horse in the entry hall. Besides, he would never wear that jacket to go up to London.

When Father did go up to London to speak or read on the BBC (he had an excellent, deep, sonorous reading voice), his travel expenses were, of course, paid. Wearing a dark formal suit and Fedora, he would take a taxi to the station. His beard would be neatly trimmed and while he certainly smelled of his pipe tobacco, he did not smell of fish. When the taxi driver knew it was for the BBC, he would come with his 1930 Rolls Royce, which he had bought second-hand for weddings – but the BBC was as grand as any local wedding. Later, he took to bringing a more modest vehicle to the house over our rocky, potholed track and transferred to the Rolls (for the last two miles) once they reached the asphalt public road. Everyone listened to the one or two wavelengths available on the radio and when Father was speaking, it was a great source of local pride: "Lu-u-u-vely voice he has," they'd say afterwards, "very profound." I'm not sure they ever discussed content, but the sound of his voice impressed them.

These dramatic occasions of his departures for London cClub – the United Universities Club), helped bolster his reputation in my mind as a Great Man, a genius much larger than life. A man to be revered, if not actually feared.

Once, he found himself sharing his railway compartment with our neighbour, the philosopher, Bertrand Russell. After a passionate discussion, Father invited Russell to join him in the dining car for luncheon. Russell (a very lively little spare man, already in his eighties) joined him readily, but only drank a glass of water, eating nothing. He explained that for some years he had been suffering from a nervous condition that made swallowing very difficult, if not impossible – he could only eat liquefied food in private. Their conversation continued as animatedly as ever all the way to London.

Another time, Father went to the dining car alone and was about to indulge in his favourite escapist literature: Agatha Christie. He opened the book, only to find the hero sitting alone in a railway dining car and opening a book... by Father! He felt a frisson of fear and *déja vu*, then tucked into his meal and the book.

We had one large bathroom (the W.C. next door) in which Father had installed an enormous bathtub on the theory that his five offspring could all be bathed together in one jolly stew. It was large enough to completely engulf him and his six foot one or two. He had not thought of the prudery that comes with adolescence (his studies of children stopped at that age), but nevertheless, there was a relaxed atmosphere amongst us and while my sisters washed, I might bathe or while my brother was shaving and singing in German (he studied modern languages), my sisters might be bathing. It was not a very practical arrangement, but everything works until it doesn't. There was also an enormous airing cupboard which housed the uninsulated copper hot water tank (heated by the small coke boiler in the kitchen). That was the only really dry place in the house, and sheets and towels were kept there – but the mattresses upon which we made our beds were always a little damp, so how long could a sheet remain dry?

That bath recalls an older sister supervising my evening bath. She is musical and sang like a lark, such tender, comforting lullabies as: "Hush-a-bye baby, Hush quite a lot, Bad babies get rabies and have to be shot," or again: "Bye baby bunting, Daddy's gone a' hunting, Gone to get a rabbit skin to wrap my baby bunting in..." But that was nothing to the time I was staying in some grand house with a starched old nursemaid who told me that if I didn't behave, she'd send "Old Boney to get me"... a reference to Napoleon Bonaparte, that frightful foreign bogeyman. She also threatened to set the Nazis with their spring-loaded heels on me (she said the springs allowed them to jump from one side of the street to the other to capture naughty children and eat them alive). At least that was a little more up to date than threatening me with Napoleon!

I probably do not recall, but have been reminded since, that one day, when the long dining room table was filled with more or less august guests, I came in very pleased with my exploits. I had very curly blond, almost white, hair and I had discovered the delights of clambering to the top of the coal pile in the coal shed and then jumping down and rolling in the coal. I recounted excitedly: "Owain, climb, jump, r-o-l-l in the coal. Fun. Happy." I was, of course black from head to foot and caused great hilarity at the lunch table. No doubt I was as mischievous as any four-year-old.

There is a family photograph (taken in 1948) of an afternoon tea party around the same table. I recognise the architects Maxwell Fry and Jane Drew in their forties. My youngest sister, sitting next to our Father and while everyone else turns cooperatively towards the camera, is in the process of stealing a piece of cake from our Father's plate next to her! My blond curls having been washed since the coal incident, I am watching her subterfuge from across the table, no doubt making a mental note for the next opportunity I might have for myself.

This house, this home, this chrysalis that gave birth to the 'me'… it was sparing on creature comforts, such as heat and light. For years we were all accustomed to climbing into beds that were not just cold, but also damp. It was not a fuzzy place, swaddled in fitted carpets, curtains and chintzes. It was unpadded, though in no way barren. Quite unobstructed, it was decorated with the fanciful originality of my Parents. Whatever influence that chrysalis (or, for that matter, my own Parents) had upon my upbringing – this is what it was.

V

FIRESIDE TALES

A round the house was a garden enclosed by a stone wall. Behind the house, on the east side, was a dark and gloomy clump of Ilex or Holm Oaks, evergreens with particularly dark green foliage. To the north, two terraces with stone walls faced the estuary – the lower one partially flooded by exceptionally high spring tides. Also on the lower one, was a well that we used whenever the mains water failed for some reason. Inside, it was lined with brick. For many years (until Father got around to having the blacksmith make some large, strap hinges), there was no cover, just a few rotted planks lay over the top like a trap for a wild animal.

We had a penny farthing – one of those ancient bicycles with a tiny back wheel and a five or six-foot wheel in front. Father had bought it at an auction, but it was left outside to slowly rust away. Before it did so, numerous of my sisters' suitors tried their best to ride the beast, no doubt in the hopes of capturing an admiring heart in the process. They all fell off very quickly, which makes one admire those cyclists of the nineteenth century who so nonchalantly peddled along in their tweed caps and britches. These regular accidents inspired a family myth: We told numerous guests that there had been a fourth daughter in the family, called Molly. She had been cycling (on the penny farthing) down the hill from the farm, when she lost control and fell into the well. When guests asked with alarm: "Was Molly badly hurt?" We would reply that she made such a noise down there that we pulled the cover over the well and laid a quartz boulder on it to stop her getting out. Clearly, the guests did not really listen to the details, for many of them continued to ask concerned questions about the sister and how her death affected us all!

Strangely, without our knowing it, this 'Molly' daughter corresponded to a child that Mother was told: "It would not be advisable to bear to term". Her pregnancy was terminated, though she regretted it forever, saying that "this child might have been the most wonderful of all of us."

As a matter of fact, this fictitious tale of *schadenfreude* was almost acted out by me, though I don't know if the accident was before or after the hatching of the myth by my older siblings: I was delighted when I inherited my brother's small bicycle (I was perhaps seven at the time) that had been brought up from our pre-War home in Laugharne. During the war, the tyres had rotted, but then, learning to ride, I would be on grass. Although the driveway was long, it was far too rocky and potholed to learn to ride a bicycle. Finally one day I managed to coast down the grass hill from the lawn in front of the house, past the 'fatal' well and around to the right at the bottom. I was so thrilled that I even burst in on Father as he worked and asked both my Parents to come out and watch. He cannot have been deeply engaged, for he came outside with his slightly sardonic smile and watched with Mother as I launched myself on the bicycle down the hill again. This time, since the gate to the left at the bottom of the slope was open, I decided to turn left instead of right. I did quite well, turned to the left through the gate at the bottom, but failed to make the turn quite sharply enough. Instead of riding triumphantly off to the left after the gate, I missed the turn and rode over the five-foot seawall and crashed onto the sharp rocks below.

I was certainly not dead, but quite bloody enough to render lurid the warm bathwater into which Mother had put me. I remember sitting in the pink water and continuing to bawl. Well, who would not want to milk sympathy for every-thing possible? Anyway, I was not at the bottom of the well and healed quickly. I soon became a more proficient bicycle rider.

Tyres were not in my primitive lexicon so the soap box car I made for myself, using the wheels off the bicycle and two others were also tyre-less. Coasting down the rocky track from the farm at the top of the hill above our house with a cousin behind me, we capsized and he somehow ran over my hand – which henceforth sported a twin track cut where one of the wheels, without a tyre, had run over me. I did not even lose the finger, so I suppose it was 'just one of those things'.

On the higher terrace to the north of the house, was a splendid solid brass cannon. It first arrived on its wooden carriage, but that quickly rotted away. Someone tried to make another carriage out of heavy, solid wood – but that too rotted away in no time. Finally, it was simply propped up on the low wall of the terrace – weighing several hundred pounds, it was unlikely to be moved until we finally sold the house.

West of the house, there lay Father's principal garden, fenced against rabbits. Southwest of the house was a line of enormous Hydrangeas on a bank, which seemed to bloom all summer long. They were amazingly dense, healthy and huge: about fifteen feet high and wide with both light and dark blue flowers, besides various pinks – all the size of a dinner plate. The entrance gate was to one side of this great barrier of blossoms, on the other side of the gate was a giant fuchsia, a small tree of a shrub, covered in red and purple pendant flowers for months on end, late into the autumn. On the lawn in front of the house, two poplars with their shiny bark stood slender and sculptural, bending in obeisance before the winter storms.

A couple of hundred yards west along the coast, my Parents had bought a square stone house on a bluff. When they were alone in winter, they often went to live there, finding it easier to heat than the large main house. They sometimes lent it to deserving young artist friends 'to finish their *magnum opus*', when they themselves went away to work in Spain, Italy or Greece during the winter. In the summer, they would rent it out to acquaintances for their summer holidays. One family in particular came back every year and still does, sixty years later. The path that led to this house passed through a small gate and up through a wet, shaded gully with blackberry brambles on either side. At night, these thorny plants would grab at one's trouser legs if one wandered ever so slightly to one side or the other in the dark. These brambles gave birth to the myth of the 'Bramble Fairies' who would reach out with their thorny briars and grab you in the night and carry you off to their lair. Again, many a child believed us implicitly when we told them about the Bramble Fairies.

It also happened that the stove in this other house (a bottled gas one) had an enormous oven. Some years later, the Christmas turkey was too large for our normal Aga oven, so it was put in the oven 'next door' (actually a quarter mile away, past the gauntlet of the Bramble Fairies). After the requisite time, I was sent to bring it back. There was a rare blizzard blowing (though the snow was not settling), the air was full of driving white fluff. I carried back the monster under a huge silver cover with the coat-of-arms of Mother's family, the snow swirling around me and almost completely covering any light from the sky. As I passed the bramble fairies, they reached out with their pointed talons and tried to drag me from the path – but I struggled on heroically with my sacred task of bringing home the roasted Christmas turkey.

I have not yet described the back stairs: They ran in a single, straight flight from the scullery up to a long passage-way upstairs. Off this passage there were doors to bedrooms, the attic and the bathroom. Both stair and corridor were floored with the original, institutional brown linoleum. This meant that when our Parents were out and it was too rainy or cold to be out-of-doors, we could play the most raucous games. One was to take a single-sized mattress and toboggan down the back stairs on it; it felt like riding a caterpillar and one finished up at the bottom in a pile, often with the mattress on top. Another version for sliding down the stairs was sitting in a large metal tub that our ducks used to bathe in – and no, we had not cleaned it out very well beforehand. This led to many smashed fingers and severe bruises, so we soon abandoned it for a softer vehicle, like the mattress.

The best game, though, involved the dogs. We played tag running up the front stairs, down the passage, down the back stairs and helter skelter through the kitchen or telephone room. The dogs would follow the chase in a general hysteria, skidding out of control when taking the sharp turns on slippery linoleum where their claws could get no purchase. They would bark excitedly, encouraging us to run faster and get wilder. Then there was a new adaptation of the game: two of my sisters received children's scooters as gifts. The chasers were each handicapped by having to stay in physical contact with a scooter, whether riding it or just dragging it along. Once they tagged someone, they would hand over the scooter and become one of the pursued.

These raucous games only became really dangerous when grown-ups joined in. Grown-ups tend to get seriously over-excited... I remember the celebrated British architect Maxwell Fry vaulting over the banister from one flight of the front stairs to the one below, still clutching his obligatory scooter and hallooing all the way. How he didn't break a leg is a mystery, he must have been well into his fifties...

I believe these games originated in Mother's mother's house, a huge Victorian pile (though the old Jacobean façade had been kept behind it, the vast house had been rebuilt in the mid-nineteenth century) of grandeur with its butler and head gardener and dozens of minions. These games were invented by adults after long, too-formal dinners. At least we had no servants to disapprove of us and our Parents didn't care (providing, of course, that they were out and could not hear the din) as long as we did not irreparably damage the house or ourselves.

There was also a much quieter game that could be equally thrilling: Cat and Mouse. Chairs and other obstructions were removed from around the long dining table and two people were chosen as Cat and Mouse. They were placed blindfolded at opposite ends of the table in stockinged feet and utter silence was declared. They moved to and fro with fingertips lightly touching the table for guidance, the cat intent on catching the mouse that was intent on survival. The tension for both the players and public was intense – especially since, on a calm night, there would not be a sound outside to distract the players. All you could hear on a still night with the tide out was the pounding of your own heartbeat in your own ears. Breathing made too much noise. Again adults tended to spoil the game by becoming over-excited and suddenly dashing at their quarry with a clatter.

Evenings, after washing the dinner dishes (which involved considerable story-telling and jokes), often closed with one person reading out loud to the rest, using one of the few Aladdin paraffin lamps with bright asbestos mantles. They were the only source of light strong enough by which to read. We huddled, cold, in front of the living room fire. The black lab, Lanta, would sit so close to the fire that her black chest was too hot to touch and, like us, her back was cold as she sat on the balding lion skin. I remember readings from many books, in particular *Englebrecht, the Surrealist Boxer* which was a favourite. We read Tolkien's *The Hobbit* in first edition, then, as soon as it was published volume by volume, there was *The Lord of the Rings*, which was reviewed by Father – somehow there was always something to read which would appeal to young and old alike, even a hilariously funny film script Father was working on for Ealing Studios.

Father would smoke his pipe or perhaps a cigar. Mother would sometimes puff on a cigar as well, but Father tired of her puffing on his good cigars with so little real pleasure, so he bought her some cheap Spanish cheroots. They were long and thin, irregular and lumpy from poor manual fabrication – and they came with woodworms in them. When the worms managed to find their way out through the skin of the cigar, the hole made it impossible to draw on them because air leaked through the holes. She never remarked on the taste of the burning worms, surely very bitter – if the worms in salad are any indication.

Besides reading out loud, there was storytelling, often by Father. He complained that when he told a story to one member of the family, the story would make the rounds of everyone else, until it finally came back to him – by which time it was totally unrecognizable. At least, by telling stories to most of us assembled in front of the fire, we all heard the same story once and for all… though when we then repeated them to school friends, we surely adapted it as much as we wished.

When Father was a teenager boarding at Charterhouse (1913-18), his dormitory was right next door to his house-master's bathroom. Every morning, winter and summer, he would be awakened at 6 a.m. by the sound of his housemaster taking his daily ice-cold bath. He would hear the old man berating himself with: "Come along now Jenks, come along now Jenks, be a man, be a man, BE A MAN!" and there would be a loud splash as he plunged into the freezing water. I have often wondered if he did it to steel his character (as in dousing his morning erection) or to cure his arthritis – both, I believe, popular reasons at the time for this Spartan habit.

I remember Father telling exotic tales of Morocco in the 1920s, his voice low and growly with pipe tobacco. How he bought his house in the Kasbah of Tangier, just down the street from his old friend Jim Wylie who had moved there even before the First World War. He told us how he had paid for the tiny house: with two donkey loads of silver, picked up from a reputable British Bank in town. The 'street' to his house, only a few meters from Place de la Kasbah, was too narrow for a fully-laden donkey with panniers to pass. So they unloaded the panniers and carried them between two men to his future house, where the seller spent thirty-six hours, cross-legged on the ground, biting every single piece to assure himself that it was indeed pure silver. Much later, post Second World War, it was on Place de la Kasbah that Barbara Woolworth Hutton restored her palace (Dar Sidi Hosni), so notorious for wild parties.

Father described how, in the 1930s, his faithful servant, Hammed, was an hereditary saint who assured Father that as a Moslem, he could not drink alcohol but he was so saintly that, if he did ever let wine pass his lips, it would turn to the "purest of water". Father told us that when Hammed joined him for a glass of wine or two, that it was interesting to note that this 'purest of waters' ingested by his faithful servant, had nevertheless a similar effect on Hammed as wine would have on other men. His servant assured him that it was definitely water that he ingested, and fervently agreed that it was remarkable that it had such an effect upon him! Another candle would now be guttering and the little coal fire would need a prod to revive it.

He also recounted how Ibn Battuta was born in Tangier in 1304 and died there in 1368 after making his famous tour of the Islamic world. Later, while still in my teens, I acquired a translation of Ibn Battuta's travels and used them as a travel guide for the few thousand miles that I myself accomplished… a drop in the ocean beside his 75,000 miles, which included southern India (which had recently converted from Buddhism to Allah) and made himself unpopular with the local rulers when he complained about the way the local women wore only a sarong, baring their breasts for all to see. Times change and now it's the Hijab in question! Ibn Battuta started out as a wealthy man and initiated a few families along the way. His journeys included similar frustrations to my own: such as revolutions, the plague, robbery, attempted rape and so on, but I admit that he had a great deal more staying power than I.

Another of Father's stories was about camping in the cork woods south of Tangier and offering passing travellers hospitality for the night in exchange for the story of their life. He talked of going pig-sticking in the desert brush. He rode a lively little Arab pony that could skip out of the way of a wild boar like the best of matadors and kept him perfectly safe – providing, of course, that he could keep his seat. Had he fallen, his long lance would have been useless against a charging boar and their great tusks would have made short work of him. The last candle would be guttering by now as Mother announced it was time for bed, saying that everyone was "getting tired and cross" (meaning herself), but small wonder that some of us caught the travel bug and especially a fascination for the adventure of visiting Muslim lands. Every time I returned from travelling in the Middle East or North Africa via Greece, I always felt I had returned home when I landed there.

Mind you, Mother was never very enamoured of Tangier. I believe she thought, although many of her best friends were gay, that it was all a bit of a waste of manhood. With homosexuality still being illegal in England (a friend was arrested in the fifties), many gays went to Tangier at the time. Besides, there was the pervasive use of hashish, while she preferred wine. Part of her distaste certainly sprang from the fact that she was operated on for appendicitis on the kitchen table of a local doctor, while several months pregnant with my brother. Both survived, but the experience put her off Morocco for good. Nevertheless, she cooked the best Moroccan tagine (on a kerosene Aladdin stove, which mimicked the very slow fire of a carefully-tended charcoal or manure fire) I have ever tasted, in Morocco or anywhere. It was the servant/saint Hammed's first wife who had taught her.

Father had also travelled to the New World, telling us of one trip he made travelling steerage (or deck class) in the early twenties with Immigrants to America and landing at Ellis Island, only to be rescued from Immigration by not one, but two limousines and their chauffeurs, sent to meet him by the fathers of friends from Oxford! Or about his trip from New York to Louisiana in an old Model T Ford. There he stayed with a most hospitable lady who he later assured me would surely be delighted if I were to call. In 1971 I decided to look her up, but found that her address had changed and she had moved, but she insisted by letter that she would be very happy to meet me – she was indeed a Grand Dame of Southern charm, now ninety nine years old and living in a genteel old people's home!

In Louisiana, Father had met an old negro who had been born a slave. The man showed him how to flip a fully-grown, sleeping alligator onto its back using a long, pointed fence-post. Then he scratched the animal's belly with the fence post, until it relaxed into a blissful state with a 'smile' on its face! And an old lady, likewise born a slave, who still lived on the impoverished plantation where she had been brought up and was now looked after by the white family that still owned it. They surprised him by calling her from her shack for lunch by yelling: "Hey Virg, dinner's ready!" When he asked about the name, he was told she was christened: Virgin Mary Queen Victoria – and you could hardly call out that mouthful! Again, small wonder that we were all imbued with wanderlust...

Then, there was the tale of how, in 1925, to save a lady-friend from some unwanted attention, he suggested to the suitor (who possessed a large, six-cylinder motor car) that they drive up north into Canada and see how far they could go. By main force, they dragged the monstrous motor further north than any automobile had ever gone before (to Lake St John) and were thanked by the local mayor with the offer of a week with a Native American tribe that was moving to their summer camp. He was astonished by the lack of verbal communication amongst the Native Americans: discussion was conducted with the slightest of hand motions and an occasional grunt. Hunters do not gossip, they are as silent as their prey.

I recall one incident during a story-telling session, Father was telling us about his wanderings in Croatia in the early 20s, when my brother and oldest sister were sitting on the floor, or more likely, on the almost bald lion skin in front of the fire. My brother was wearing an ancient pair of lace-up shoes, perhaps second-hand ones. They had been repaired with new soles that ended at his instep or arch of his foot. There, they had been nailed together, but the glue had failed and if he curled his toes up in a particular way, a gap opened like a mouth in the sole of his instep. However, when the 'mouth' opened, it displayed the line of small tack nails that had not held, like tiny shark's teeth. In the faint light of the fire, my sister saw the gap in his sole and decided to try tickling his stockinged foot inside – in the dim light she did not see the tiny nails. When she got in her first little tickle, he automatically arched his foot away from the annoyance and she screamed like a banshee, her fingers grabbed by the serried rank of sharp nails. The interruption brought the proceedings to an abrupt halt, until we all understood how the trap had been sprung and laughed it all away.

VI

POSTWAR SURVIVAL / BABY SITTERS

As soon as I was old enough, it was my job to wash out the fragile glass chimneys of the lamps, using soapy water to remove the soot. I trimmed the wicks straight and sometimes changed them or the asbestos mantles which came with a protective pink coating on it that you burned off with a match. Thereafter it was fragile as a worm cast in sand. Then I filled the lamps with kerosene from a small hand pump, ready for the evening's reading.

Besides the four ducks (whose bath we purloined to slide down the stairs), we had four chickens that had a very nice little hen house, which we kept scrupulously clean. As they grew older, instead of laying fewer and fewer eggs, they laid more and more. Finally the mystery was solved: young free-range hens from the farm two fields away would come and lay their eggs in our hen house. When the old girls finally went in the stew pot, we were careful to keep the hen house just as clean, with fresh straw in the laying boxes. But alas the neighbour's chickens no longer came... we decided that it was the conversation of the old hens that brought in neighbouring chickens, not so much their fancy clean house.

At one time, there was such a menagerie at the house, that when Mother went away and we were all off at school, it was quite a task for Father to take care of them all by himself. He solved the logistical problem with porridge – raw oats for the horses and the white rabbit (his oats were mixed with used tea leaves, which he loved) and cooked porridge for himself, besides the two grown dogs, seven puppies (bred from Lanta), a cat called Michew (from *micino* – pussycat), four ducks, four hens and the jackdaw with a crossed beak called Dr Marara Douglas (had to be an honourable 'doctor', since we never knew what sex it was). So 'everyone' ate porridge.

Dr Marara had been saved from under its nest by my middle sister, who wanted to be a veterinarian. It could not eat properly because of its deformity, so we kept it in the fruit cage in the garden. Jackdaws are not very interested in soft fruit and we fed it well on things like porridge and tiny scraps of our food. It used to sit on my sister's shoulder during tea, but never did learn to talk – as they are reputed to do. Finally, it seemed to manage on its own and we let it go. For two or three years thereafter, it would come back to visit us, accompanied by a spouse… but in the end must have decided that we were not worth the trouble.

Talking of birds, Father took the foghorn from the *Tern* (our largest boat, at 25 feet) and fixed it to a post that held one end of our washing line. We could all be summoned to meals with a good loud, lugubrious 'honk' on the horn. Its sound carried for miles. One evening, he was dining at Portmeirion Hotel opposite and met a celebrated ornithologist who remarked on the strange honk he heard from time to time on the estuary. That certainly showed to what extent we did not live by the clock. Meals were never at regular times, so the timing of the foghorn's honk was pretty much aleatory.

Indeed, Mother always had a great deal of trouble with numbers – as with times, cheque books and the like. Father used to say that if he wrote another bestseller he would have a watch surgically implanted on Mother's wrist. He did (write another bestseller) but did not (carry through with his threat).

A helpful little nephew came into the kitchen one day and asked if he might help.

"Why, yes!" she replied, "go and lay the table."

"For how many people?" he queried.

"Oh, I don't know – a *lot*! Don't ask stupid questions."

Another time, another child asked her if he might help with the cooking?

"Go and break six eggs."

A few minutes later, he came back with: "Auntie, I've broken them for you."

"Where are they?"

"On the larder floor."

"Oh you bloody fool. I wanted them in a bowl. Go and clean them up at once." He did so, using one of those push carpet cleaners with revolving brushes…

When chaos was getting the better of Mother, she would start singing a hymn that went: "Confusion rains where'er the sun, doth his successive journeys run…" I felt it was not so appropriate when it had been pouring with rain for so long. Though I am sure it was precisely at those times that Mother became overwhelmed because the house would be too full of children moping around. Then she had no space to think.

There were clearly times when us smaller children were in the way and had to be disposed of or farmed out. The older ones could well fend for themselves, but my youngest sister and I were twice dropped off at hotels as the easiest method of having a baby-sitter – in the form of hotel staff. I suppose that we were relatively well behaved and tractable as children go, but children lack the experience of life that can help avoid some accidents.

Once we were dropped at the fabulous Portmeirion Hotel, that architectural folly blending salvaged ancient buildings, Italianate cottages and Chinese pagodas made of sheet steel. The manager was an old friend of Father's from Tangier, Jim Wylie. Jim was a lively, witty man, a homosexual painter, who had moved to Tangier around 1908. He used to drive up through Spain and France to England every spring to his summer job as hotel manager. He did landscape paintings along the way and until very late in life insisted on driving all the way in an Austin Healey Sprite (the one with bug-eye headlights) loaded with small canvasses and paints. Anyone who knows the tiny car may judge his intrepid eccentricity.

One day, he was entertaining grown-ups with cocktails and his incredible stories on the hotel lawn, when a furious older lady came running across the grass, clad in slippers and nightgown, with her hair in curlers: "Mr Wylie, Mr Wylie, there's a cockroach in my bath!" He leapt to his feet with agility that belied his age and rushed towards her, crying: "Oh, how exciting Mrs So-and-so, is it all right? I've never seen a cockroach in my life! Will you please show it to me?" This, after some fifty years in Tangier, where if there isn't a cockroach in your bathroom, it's because you don't have a bathroom.

Another time, we were dropped at the Oakley Arms near Maentwrog, nowadays a rather dour pub. When I was put into my musty, damp bed (where was my youngest sister, I think she was there?) I amused myself by tearing up little strips of paper, dipping them in my water glass and applying them to the bulb of my reading light to hear the hiss. Since I was too young to use it for reading, the hissing sound that ensued, seemed a delightful use of the thing. Until the bulb exploded, showering shards of thin glass everywhere.

The rest of the time at the hotel, and indeed for some years after (perhaps even to this very day), I lived in mortal dread of being called to task for my sabotage, perhaps sent to prison or chained to the oar of a galley or even burned at the stake like Joan of Arc. Oh yes, Mother had taught me a lot about *la Sainte Jeanne*.

Less intimidating, despite being alone, was the elderly widow who still farmed her smallholding just twenty minutes' walk above the old Parc house in the mountains. Mrs. Lloyd-Williams was a determined powerhouse. She went about the tasks on her farm, Garth-y-foel, with the slow deliberation of an old-time farmer, now handicapped by arthritis and general old age. She was wise beyond comprehension and people often sought her out for advice. She had a craggy, deeply-lined, smiling face. She put me in the guest room of the farmhouse, which had been furnished for her wedding in the 1920s. The sheets were spotless, if a little worn – my foot went through a hole in the bottom sheet and I thought I had lost it forever. The hot water bottle I was given to warm my bed was indeed a bottle: a large, bulbous, ceramic bottle (that weighed its size in stone, it was so thick) with a cork stopper. My elderly hostess had filled this ceramic bottle with boiling water.

I carried the bottle upstairs and carefully put it where I would be lying in the bed. I covered it again and went downstairs for tea (the worker's evening meal) in the kitchen. There was something very wise and deeply kind about Mrs Lloyd-Williams, her unused parlour spoke of genteel origins. The china on the dresser and slender furniture recalled finer times. But I always remembered her thick red arms, the sleeves rolled up to her elbows as she taught me to milk the cows by hand. I once met her at some occasion, perhaps a funeral, dressed in her best black, with big black feathers in her black hat. I ran to hide from this unknown grand lady.

Back upstairs, the spot where I had placed the hot water bottle was too hot to sit on, so I slid it around to chase back the damp cold of the rest of the bed. It was a high bed (perhaps a four-poster?) and took some climbing to get in. I fell asleep fast enough, but was awakened by a terrible crash: it was the hot water bottle, now totally cold, that I had pushed away with my feet and it had fallen to the floor. I imagined it cracking open and pouring its contents of cold water all over the wooden floor planks. I had made as awful a gaffe as I had when playing with water on the light bulb at the Oakley Arms Hotel. I fell back to sleep anyway.

In the morning, the ceramic bottle was intact and my hostess never mentioned the great thump in the night. She awakened me early to help with the milking. She treated me like an adult, albeit a 'city' adult who needed to learn the ropes. She had already fed the cows and mucked out the cowshed and washed it down with disinfectant. My hands were neither large enough, nor strong enough, to be much use in milking, but I learned quickly, and proudly milked two whole cows by myself, while she did the other six and lots of other things besides.

We went inside for breakfast and after that she showed me how to churn the milk to make butter. She made most of her milk into butter because it was not worth the trouble of carrying her very few gallons to Parc, to be picked up by the farmer there and taken down to be then picked up by the dairy to be bottled. These were still the days before milk coolers (she had no electricity) and pasteurization. Thus, she sold whatever small amount of milk had been ordered, the rest went to making butter. With fewer and fewer farms still making butter, hers sold well.

She had a large wooden barrel with a crank handle on a cradle. She poured the milk in and then started to turn the crank. I remember marvelling at those strong arms going round and round for what seemed like hours on end. She told me to try, but I could last only a few minutes before giving up in exhaustion. When she was satisfied with the consistency, she would pour off the whey, which some customers even preferred to whole milk (I suppose this buttermilk is more like low-fat milk) and put the butter into moulds and stamped them with her butter stamp in the form of a thistle. I was used to eating shop-bought butter which came from New Zealand at the time, it was bright yellow with food colouring rather than natural carotene, while the butter made by Mrs Lloyd Williams was pure white, white as lard or shortening. She did not salt it as the Bretons do, to help in preserving it and there were beads of sweated water on the surface.

Father, when he was lucky enough to buy a pound of her butter, would salt it himself... as for hers, the demand was such that she never had to worry about conserving it without refrigeration. By now, most of her clients had electricity and refrigerators and could thus keep the unsalted butter for weeks.

Of course, one problem in the equation that had been dealt with from time immemorial, was that there were no telephones in the Croesor Valley. She could not call clients to say the butter or the milk was ready, nor could they enquire. The only method of communication was to 'stop by', which, if she was not too busy, entailed a cup of tea and the local news. Indeed, when my Parents wanted to invite a guest from the mountains to dinner, they had to send a telegram to the Post Office in Garreg and hope that someone would walk down the two or three miles from where they lived and then back up again, dropping off urgent messages such as telegrams on the way. If the telegram required a response, then the recipient would have to walk down to the Post Office where there was a telephone box and there they could make the call to us, accepting or declining. It was a most laborious form of bush telegraph. A few people now had cars, and that made the trip much easier, but ownership of a car entailed a good deal of community service as well... as in: "We'll be needing your car to take Gran to the doctor next Tuesday." Wealth had its concomitant responsibilities.

The alternative to staying with Mrs Lloyd-Williams or in a local hotel was less appealing, because it bore with it far more solicitous care than I was accustomed to, besides more rules. That was going to stay with Uncles and Aunts. They all lived in England and their spouses had normal jobs such as banking or farming. I never went to stay with Mother's Brother until much later. He was a brilliant eccentric whose letters to *The Times* were regularly published. He was a pioneer in ecological farming and used some of the very first solar panels in Britain. His four children were younger than we and his beautiful Spanish wife (who had worked as a translator throughout the war) knew, I believe, her limits as to how many small children she could manage at any one time. Their house was always a delightful chaos, not unlike our own, yet very different in its muddle.

This uncle and aunt came to stay with us from time to time and if either was under the weather, they both retired to bed and ate nothing until they both felt better. She always had just the right tool in her handbag for any small repairs that might come up. We saved up broken twelve-volt table lights and egg timers for this aunt to repair when she came.

* * *

The Banker Uncle (by marriage, the one whose courtship caused my grandmother to call him 'A counter-jumper'), on the other hand, was very tall and kind. He treated me as his equal – which left me swimming in completely unknown waters. The Farmer Uncle (also by marriage) was kind enough and jolly, though with him I was clearly a child. In both cases, I was bewildered by the regular, excessive meals, which seemed to take up the whole day, when one could have been off catching tadpoles or fishing for minnows in the stream.

There was always breakfast with cereal, eggs and bacon and sausages and fried tomatoes, and toast and marmalade... Then came luncheon with overcooked meat and overcooked vegetables and a bland salad and some pudding. Tea entailed little cups and saucers with milk jug and sugar bowl and little spoons and tiny sandwiches and scones and cakes. Dinner, included an *hors d'oeuvre*, more meat or fish and vegetables (forever, over-cooked), a salad and desert. The rhythm suffocated me, though I followed it politely.

The banker's hobby and expertise had led him to become Chairman of the British Numismatic Society. He never spoke of his business day. But he did show me a little 'valueless' coin in his collection that amused him: it had been minted in the very village to which he had moved, by the local grocer or perhaps the general store. What amused him about it was that the merchant's family name was the same as his own. The fact that it was minted in about 1450 gave it no great value, he told me. In those days, the King minted sovereigns (and no one else might do the same), but there was no small change available. A sovereign was a year's pay for a labourer. So the local store minted their own change which was probably only viable at that store... the very origin of the 'company store'. This uncle was very tall, slender and courtly.

The Farmer was a little more corpulent, and much shorter. He walked with a rolling limp from too many broken legs and hips as a horse trainer before the War. He was always in a good mood and had the fattest, the healthiest, the best pigs, sheep and cattle. He ran his farm with great efficiency and was always beamingly proud of his crops, his stock and his children. He was also a mine of child-friendly funny stories and anecdotes, which he recounted in his jolly fast voice and then laughed at with more gusto than did we. He was treasurer of his church and was once pounced upon after a service by a large lady of the congregation:

"Mr Treasurer, you have not sent me a receipt for my generous contribution."

"Oh dear" he replied, "when did you send it? What kind of envelope was it in?"

"Three weeks ago in one of those small brown business envelopes."

"Well, that explains it! I take quite a while to open brown envelopes, they usually contain bills."

Both of these kind Uncles and Aunts had what Mother referred to as: 'conventional homes', with lots of little tables piled with knickknacks, tiny china figurines and silver whatsits. They were what I would call, 'overstuffed houses'. No place for toddlers, but I was a discreet boy by then, I wore a tie to dinner and attempted conversation with my neighbours at table. It was like being in prison for me... I far preferred to be out on the salt marshes with my dog or walking the hills.

These were just a sample of my general hosts, when my

Parents could no longer put up with my existence... Mother once told me that, after a long luncheon with some relatives of their generation, Father said (as he turned the car out of their driveway): "Can you imagine? They have children! That means that they must have, at some time, disrobed and had intimate relations!" Yes, some of them were most definitely, *Formal!*

If there was one thing Mother despised, it was conventionality – her greatest compliment was always: 'original'. She loved her sisters, but it was despite their profound conventionality and really, they were much easier to deal with than her eccentric younger brother. They came when they said they would, they always had money in the bank and they could be counted upon to take in any of her children when she didn't know what to do with us. Our cousins often came to stay with us and loved the unstructured, barefoot chaos of our lives, but I am sure the logistics of arranging for them to come must have been quite terrifying to their regimented parents!

A pair of very young twin cousins were sent to stay with us alone by train. Their mother asked them if they would recognise the stop where they were supposed to get out. "Oh yes," said one: "it's the station which has a tap with a notice saying 'Not Drinking Water'!" All train stations in Britain had taps with that warning on them...

VII

GRANNY CADOGAN

Then there were the Christmases that we did not spend in London amongst 'intellectuals', when we went to stay with Mother's mother (Granny Cadogan, née Howard, first married to Bazley, Mother's father) for the holiday. She no longer lived in the enormous Jacobean/Victorian mansion where she had brought up her own family, by now that had been converted into a girl's private school. She had moved to a much more modest old rectory... but modest? Oh how some country vicars had lived!

The house seemed to have a dozen bedrooms, huge living room, elegant dining room, besides vast kitchens and coach houses around a courtyard, all built of that warm, honey-coloured stone so typical of the Cotswolds. A lovely lazy river (right out of *The Wind In The Willows*) dozed brilliantly clear and full of water life, through the garden. Grandmother was old. She was virtually blind and wore a too-tidy white wig. She sat regally in her throne-like chairs and ran the household in its minutest detail. When she left one of her thrones and walked very slowly with two canes, then she became poignantly mortal. She was a staunch teetotaller, though she paid for her husband's pleasure in good wines and spirits, besides that of all her guests. She did not impose her beliefs.

On Christmas Day 1954, the enormous glass-like mahogany table had been set with her finest lace, cut crystal glasses and solid silver. Her second husband had carved the turkey with a textbook in front of him, counting out the enormous slices of over-cooked meat according to technical sketches in the book. We ate enormously, the grown-ups drank wine, but the festivity was muted, like a brewing storm that never bursts. We all knew that after lunch we would have to listen to the Queen's Speech on the wireless and not until that was over, might we open our presents. As coffee was served to the adults, liqueur chocolates were passed. No one noticed that the children all had one, and then she took one. With the first bite she knew her mistake as a teetotaller and spat it out with such force that the perfectly waxed solid mahogany table, the hand-laundered and ironed lace, the lovingly shined, sparkling silver were all splattered with wet chopped chocolate.

Granny's second husband (the first, grandson of the amazing industrialist, having died of complications from a routine appendectomy after giving her five children) was a delightful character. Known as 'the Commander', he had run away to the navy as a teenager. On a four-masted training schooner he managed to fall, not just from the masthead to the deck, but right to the bottom of the empty hold, on his head. Or so it was said. Anyway, he remained frozen at the charming, lively age of sixteen throughout his life, though with a stocky old man's build and permanent whisky breath. He enjoyed telling the story of how he had met Granny (recently widowed) in 1912.

He was commander of a British battleship laying off Boulogne and was checking out the local talent through his powerful Navy-issue binoculars, when he "espied" (his own word) "a most handsome and stately lady promenading with her brood of five children, kept in check by plenty of nurse-maids." "Damn," he would go on, in full hearing of his regal wife, "looked like a fine breeder to me, with that brood in her train. So, being a man of action, I called up the Quartermaster and ordered him to lower a longboat with eight oarsmen and take my card to the Lady. Upon presenting my compliments, he was to invite the little family for a full tour of the battle-ship."

When the longboat returned, it was full of white lace and femininity, so while the children were amused, he made his honourable intentions clear. I gather that Grandmother was enchanted, for they married and she bore him two more children, a son who died in the Second World War – another of her older sons having already died while serving as Britain's youngest Member of Parliament at the time (he was twenty-six). The second child, a daughter (widowed during World War II), served as a lady-in-waiting to Princess, then Queen, Elizabeth for her lifetime. A very beautiful, cuttingly witty and hilarious aunt.

At some point in this second marriage she gave the Commander a brand-new Bugatti. It was delivered to the stables – now being converted more and more into garages (though the Head Coachman, whose title had become Head Chauffeur, never did quite master the art of driving a horse-less carriage) and he was told to go and find it there. Delighted, he turned on the ignition, checked that it was in neutral, set the ignition advance/retard, the hand throttle, hand choke – and cranked it into life. He must have sat in it for a few minutes to warm it up, before letting off the choke, re-adjusting the spark timing and putting it into gear. He listened to the perfect little engine sing as he accelerated, shifted into gear and let in the clutch. He drove it full-tilt into the heavy stone wall at the end of the garage. I believe Bugatti rebuilt it for someone else.

Staying with Granny Cadogan was a regimented affair, with meals at precise times. I had to wear a jacket and tie for meals, though dinner jackets (or tuxedos) were only worn by older boys and for special dinners. Everything ran like clock-work, until the day when her husband (we never called him Grandfather, since he was our 'step-' and anyway we had a more affectionate name for him: Duggy) came home to lunch an hour late. The household was upset, the kitchen staff out of humour, when Duggy came waltzing in, full of enthusiasm: "Driving back from Sisister (as locals pronounced Cirencester) when a great flight of Canada geese came over. Damn, if I didn't count up to twenty-seven of them before I went into the ditch!" A farmer eventually pulled him out of the ditch with his tractor and here he was, unscathed, but late for luncheon.

He was a breath of fresh air; forever an enthusiastic sixteen-year-old, he delighted us children with his puerile conjurer's tricks, fake turds and ink spills. For the coronation of Queen Elizabeth II, in the summer of 1953, he spent days setting up a firework display using fireworks he had kept since before the war. He had nailed the fireworks to planks he had laid on a wheelbarrow, which naturally meant they were so close together that they ignited each other in one magnificent explosion which sent the wheelbarrow (rocket-propelled) into one of Granny's favourite bushes, setting it ablaze. My brother and Duggy were the only ones outside, we children and women were watching from behind a large window at a safe distance. I must have been looking away at the dramatic moment, so as far as I was concerned, the coronation celebration was a mere damp comedy of errors with barely a *bang* or a *pop*.

We watched the ceremony on television (Granny had the first one I ever saw) and it was of course black and white. Richard Dimbleby commentated historically, relating arcane technical details to fill every empty space in the long, boring proceedings. Indeed, that was my only memory of watching television until I was eighteen. My farmer uncle refused to purchase a television because he said it only showed trash... with the result that my cousins went to watch television in the cottage of his tractor driver – who was not so narrow-minded.

At Christmas time, Grandmother would hold a ball for her own children and their offspring. The carpet in the drawing room was rolled back and most of the furniture removed. We so wanted some of our second cousins, the

Howards invited, but she was adamant – no one but her direct issue and their families might attend. My sisters wore long skirts and occasionally dragged me onto the dance floor, to their embarrassment and my total confusion.

"Watch my feet, you little fool!"

"I can't see them, they're under your dress."

"Well follow my lead."

"I can't do anything else, you're stronger than me."

Later, when I was almost a teenager, Granny told me of going to balls when she was young. They were often in the winter and before the young people set off in the coach, all dressed up, her own mother would summon the Head Coachman and enquire after the condition of the roads and bridges on the way. Of course, Grandma and her siblings and friends would waylay the coachman, kiss him sweetly and implore him to report favourably on travelling conditions. Sometimes a bridge might be down, washed away by an unusual flood – in that case it would take a lot of kisses and sweet words to get the coachman to assure their mother that it would only take twenty minutes more to bypass the fallen bridge... but they did their damnedest to get to the party one way or another. As highly privileged, young people, they must have yearned for social contact, what with raging young hormones and an insular life in 'the castle'.

VIII

NICE SICILIAN MURDERER

Tonino (always known as Nino) and Theresa were young Sicilian cousins who, in 1950, came to work for my Parents in Wales. It was Nino's abounding energy that built much of the last half mile of driveway from the farmhouse to our house, without any machinery more sophisticated than a wheelbarrow, shovel and pickaxe – with only the strength of his limbs and the sweat of his brow. It was a Herculean task and the end result was still extremely rocky, wrecking the suspension of car after car. He carried coal, repaired things, and sometimes cooked dinner. He bought an old motorcycle and went home for a visit, carrying a Welsh farm cat with him. He came back again abruptly – apparently the fuss over his having killed one of his brothers in a rage had still not blown over. He played Sicilian love songs on his accordion and slicked back his black hair with olive oil – I worshipped him and nearly killed myself imitating his coiffure with water (in midwinter) – which resulted in pneumonia, of which more later.

Theresa was a skinny little peasant girl when she arrived. The first time we all sat down to eat together, she saw the large loaf of English white bread on the table and asked politely (in Sicilian Italian – in all the years she spent with us she never did learn to speak much English) how much of it she was allowed to eat. Bread was no longer rationed and indeed was probably subsidized by the Government, so

Father said she could eat as much as she wished. From that moment on, she ate a loaf at each meal. Fortunately, she was an excellent seamstress and could let in darts of any spare cloth Mother could spare her, front and back to her dresses. They stood out like lightning flashes with their variegated colours and strange shapes to accommodate her broadening figure.

She was as strong as an ox, especially when there were young men looking on – swinging a full bale of straw onto her shoulder as if it were an elegant little evening handbag. Not for her: "This is so heavy, will you please help me?" She was raised to know that men wanted good, strong, hard workers as wives, not dainty wimps.

I used to try to teach her to read in English, starting with an illustrated children's book called: *Orlando, the Marmalade Cat.* I seem to recall that progress was slow, but then, she probably did not read in Italian either.

The first time Theresa went home, she took a suitcase of practical work clothes, heavy wool stockings, shoes and boots. She was a hero. The next time she went home, she took a suitcase of nylons, heeled shoes, nylon dresses and make-up. Her father threw her out of the house. She was a hussy. After that, each time she went home, she knew what she had best take home, though, for herself, she continued to indulge in these new luxuries. Synthetic fibres were taking over the market in England as it struggled to recover from the ruinous war, but they took many more years to reach Theresa's Sicily (and Spain, Greece and Yugoslavia, for that matter). But, by then, we (in England) were looking for 100 per cent cotton again!

Father's lapses in his sketchy Italian became legendary: "Please put the dog in the oven and the horse in the colander." (Instead of *carne* – 'meat' he said *cane* – 'dog', instead of *cavalo* – 'cabbage', he said *cavallo* – 'horse'). Mother used her hands like an Italian and so got her point over more successfully.

When Nino used Father's coracle to fish for flatfish (plaice), he would lie across the thwart with its broad leather strap for carrying the boat on one's back. He would brandish a homemade spear of bamboo, with a nail in the end whose head he had removed and in which he had cut a notch to serve as a barb. In the thrill of the chase, he became over-excited and several times plunged the spear through the thin-skinned coracle, instead of the fish below. In view of his fratricidal history, Father was reluctant to let him use a gun, but I believe he relented and Tonino wasted many precious shells on harmless little birds: "Silly damn bird, I think he was a rabbit." Indeed, he was using a 16 bore repeater shotgun with a five-cartridge magazine, so one can imagine how much was left of the little thrush, once the magazine was empty!

After a few years, first Nino, then Theresa, stopped coming back from their long visits home and settled down where they were happier: the Mezzogiorna or Land of the Midday Sun. Then my Parents took to having au pair girls or young men from Switzerland, Germany and France. Even distant cousins came from Bavaria (their father had been very much on the 'other side' during the war). Our distant French cousins (though poorer than the German branch) were much too grand to come as au pairs, so they came as guests. There was one occasion when Father had been left alone at home and told to meet a Swiss girl at the railway station. The arrangements had been made by Mother but she was off somewhere for a few weeks. He met the girl and brought her home. No sooner was he home again, than the Station Master called to say there were two or three more foreign ladies and he could not understand where they were supposed to be going. He presumed they must be 'for us'.

Father drove back to the station and brought them all home, at least for the night. This occasioned his famous telegram to Mother: *"CONTINENTAL DAMSELS ARRIVING ON EVERY TRAIN stop PLEASE STOP AT SOURCE OF SUPPLY"*.

Twelve words, the minimum charge for a telegram. As it turned out, Mother had cancelled two, but they had not understood, and the third was supposed to be going to work on a farm. His French and German were much more proficient than his Italian and he soon managed to sort everything out, found homes for the two who had been refused and took the third to the farm where she was supposed to be working.

'Old Mr Edwards' was the tenant farmer of twelve poor acres on the north slope of the hill behind our house. It took him painfully long to limp the two hundred yards from his cottage to our house, bearing fresh milk and eggs in the morning. He had no milk cooler (how could he without electricity?), so the milk was still warm from the cows and the eggs from the hens. The milk would turn before teatime, so Father made cream cheese from it. He would hang a muslin bag of curds over the scullery sink, to drip its chalky water on the dishes. Mr Edwards spoke an imaginative English, in which 'The Winkies' were the lithe little weasels or stoats that lived in the dry-stone farm walls, while my sisters, when they goading their ponies to jump obstacles, he complained were: "Rushing and springing, springing and rushing, they are…" for he did not want his field chewed up by the hooves of the ponies, as they jumped their jumps. Progress had left the old man in its wake. The law required milk to be pasteurized and tuberculin-tested… he and his three old cows could not keep up. All four died, in what order, I do not know.

I still see him methodically scything six acres of hay each summer, by hand. A rhythmic slow swing of the great scythe, only interrupted to turn the hay upside down from time to time and, leaning on the crooked handle, sharpen the long, curved blade. Old Father Time. The grass cut, his one-legged son (a motorcycle accident, not the war) came for his 'holiday' to help his father turn the hay, sometimes piling it up on tepees of three posts, to keep it off the wet ground while it dried. Everyone prayed for a dry week (rare enough in Wales). Once dry enough, an ancient lorry would appear and they would cart it into his barn for the cows in winter. If stored damp, it would ferment, getting so hot it could burst into flames, consuming the year's crop along with the barn. Richer farmers had insurance and some suspected their haystack fires, but Mr Edwards was his own insurance. He worked until he could work no more and then he died.

One year, there was to be an exceptionally high spring tide and my older siblings (and, no doubt, our Mother, who was always in favour of a dramatic 'adventure') suggested we should celebrate the occasion. Everyone we knew was invited and we posted announcements in village stores and post offices in the area. The *Tern* was anchored in front of the house, where she could be spot lit by the headlights of the old Jeep. A 'pirate' attack was enacted by rowing boats attacking the '*Tern*'. Father, wearing an Army-surplus snow camouflage suit (pure white) climbed to the masthead of the *Tern* illuminated by the Jeep, no mean feat for a man in his fifties and a boat only 25 feet long. I've done it myself more recently and the boat wobbles even in the flattest calm. I recall a Lord Somebody-or-other who slipped on the same rocks that I had fallen onto on my bicycle, and broke his hip, so the police were called to help carry him up on a stretcher. After that excitement, I suppose I conked out. I was still very young for late nights.

There was also the evening when we devised a 'medieval' dinner party. We were all dressed up in suitable costumes, the young men with thick socks whose toes were tied up to their calves like medieval shoes. Someone wanted to dress me in a little velvet suit with silver buttons so then they said I looked like some wimpish character I despised. I cried until Mother told me this was nonsense, I was to be called 'Sir Firebrand' and stop bawling! Straw was laid on the floor and we used no plates or forks, just thick slabs of bread onto which pieces of roast meat were served. Of course there were knives, much jesting, grandiose toasts, boasting and wild tales of great daring. The dogs, which had been strictly raised never to beg for food at the table, played their parts as hunting dogs quite pathetically. They were supposed to stay under the table on the straw and eat the bones we threw them once we had gnawed them ourselves. But they were so well behaved that they retired to a corner of the room and sat dribbling saliva onto the floor, their backs turned to us in shocked disdain at our uncivilised behaviour.

Another dinner was organised to celebrate the visit of an 'Eastern Potentate', actually a dark-skinned young actor who was staying. He was very good-looking and had huge brown soulful eyes. One guest was a somewhat overweight teenage girl, whom he took into a corner and was heard declaring his lust for more 'well-covered virgins' for his harem. She seemed so flattered by the compliment that it became quite embarrassing – especially when she afterwards refused to believe it was a hoax! That one was not quite so kind. Later the young actor set out to cross the estuary at low tide, wearing a cloak and carrying a sword – I remember him disappearing out of his depth in the wrong place in the channel, his sword still brandished above his head crying: "Excalibur".

There was the time that the local foot Hunt was in our neighbourhood, because the farmers complained there were too many foxes. This was no elegant affair with the gentry on superb horses, all immaculately turned out – no, this was a foot pack (horses could never keep up in this rough terrain). The foxes never went to the summits of mountains, they knew they could be encircled up there, but following a hunt would often involve as much walking as it would take to scale half a dozen peaks. The technique was to watch the dogs from a vantage point and guess as to how best to cut them off. The day that the Hunt came to a neighbouring farm, Mother invited everyone to a high tea at the end. The hounds had been corralled into their trailer and there were quite few battered and muddy old Land Rovers parked in the field outside. As people worked their way through piles of sandwiches, eggs and ham and cake, there was a sudden uproar in the back yard by the coal shed. The hounds had succeeded in escaping from their trailer and had soon discovered a rubbish bin, which our own dogs were too polite to attack. In a matter of seconds, there was domestic rubbish spread across the countryside and the hounds were trying to rip each other apart, no doubt in their disappointment at the slim pickings in the rubbish. The Master of the Hounds was out in a trice, his ruddy face now puce with rage, as he bellowed and roared and lashed about with his whip. Finally, they were corralled once more, back in their trailer. I do not believe we even killed a fox that day, 'kills' were few and far between – but following the hounds was very energetic exercise and a good change to scaling mountains.

However, much of my school holidays (four months a year) were spent alone, dreaming. I would take the dogs Lanta, a black Labrador and one of my sisters' dogs Iago, for long walks down the estuary and out onto the remote salt marshes near the sea. Lanta was named after Atlanta; for some reason, it had been decided that she was very vain. She was a rather stupid, good-natured pedigree while Iago was an intelligent mongrel cross between a collie and a terrier. He was a handsome smaller dog with fluffy white breeches, a black patch 'saddle' a bit askew, and a little brown around the eyes. The two of them would chase seagulls for miles, the gulls seemed to play with them by gliding along ten feet off the ground, never far ahead of the dogs. The dogs became frantic with the 'hunt' and ran and ran. They almost never wore collars and leashes and when they did, would pull incessantly, making them cough pathetically.

Lanta was a very strong swimmer and before I learned to swim she would pull me along in water far out of my depth. She swam only with her front paws and tail, swishing it to and from to add power – her hind legs neatly curled up like the retractable wheels on an aircraft. In those days, I would stay in the water for hours on end, until I was blue – hypothermia must have been close at hand for Mother to put me in the huge bathtub all alone in the afternoon. Lanta was also an excellent diver and could swim out and dive for a heavy bone we threw for her. She had the soft mouth of her breed and enjoyed carrying my sisters' dolls around the house, never chewing on them but getting them thoroughly wet with her saliva. Diving nearly cost her her life: I took her out with a bone to dive for in mid-winter and, like me, she also caught pneumonia. I suppose there was no hot tub for her, when she got too cold. I really bonded with her as I nursed her back to health, feeding her by hand, mostly from my own plate.

Whenever Lanta was in heat, we kept her carefully locked up and sometimes tried to influence her choice of lovers with the introduction of a 'suitable' pedigree Labrador. That never worked. She always managed to escape and follow her heart to the wiry black Welsh sheep dogs so valued locally for their highly intelligent herding skills with sheep. Her offspring were much favoured by local poachers, who said her puppies were stronger than pedigree Labs. I never knew how Father came to do business with these disreputable hunters, but by the time Lanta had raised some fifty puppies, homes with poachers were running short.

I remember one old poacher particularly well for his collection of accidents, though he never got one of our puppies – Father said he was such a fool, he was bound to shoot the dog by mistake. This was not so far-fetched: he carried an old muzzle-loading shotgun that had to be loaded with a ramrod and did not use pre-packed cartridges. One day he could not remember whether or not he had loaded the gun, so he put the ramrod in to feel how far down it would go. It seemed to get a little stuck, so he gave the ramrod a smart tap with the palm of his hand. It was loaded and went off, shooting the ramrod right through his hand. When he had recovered, everyone hoped he would not be able to go shooting with only one hand, but not at all – he just became even more of a liability.

One day the fool crawled through a thick hedge, leaving

his gun on the other side, then reaching back through the gap in the hedge, he grabbed the gun by its muzzle and started to pull it through after him. A twig caught on the trigger and he shot off his own shoulder... which finally put paid to his poaching days. After that we would see him sadly gimping along his old haunts, mercifully unarmed.

The hunting around us was so poor that the landowner only had one old gamekeeper nearby. Not only did I never see him out patrolling for poachers, I have no recollection of the man. I only remember his small cottage and always gave it a wide berth. I presume we were considered sufficiently 'gentry' to have permission to hunt there, but the really poor folk who desperately needed to hunt could be prosecuted for doing so on private property (as all the land was).

When any of us shot a rabbit, we gutted it at once, on the hillside. Otherwise, there was nowhere to throw out such offal and it would have to be taken down to the tide and fed to the seagulls. Mind you, it would have been much kinder to the remaining rabbits if we had thrown out the guts on the marsh, it was thoughtless of us to leave them *in situ* where they would be discovered by their relatives. When Father shot wild duck, he hung them by the neck from a tree, without gutting them. In theory, he said, he should leave them there until they fell to the ground with rot in the neck. That was called 'hanging game'. In point of fact, every time one finally fell to the ground, it was already so full of maggots that there was no question of actually consuming it at table. I suspect that this was a medieval custom forced by the lack of refrigeration. In those days they used a very salty, spicy sauce called *Garum*, introduced by the Romans, to season and mask the taste of rotten meat. *Garum* still exists; its modern form is *Nuoc Mam Pha San*, the Vietnamese sauce made from the juice of rotted salt fish.

IX

BERSERK JEEP HITS LONDON

Sometimes I would take a large umbrella out into the middle of the estuary and sit under it on the sand, dreaming in the pouring rain. I forget of what I dreamed the most, but sex (in some warped, childish and uninformed version) and cars had a prominent place. I could not bear the wait until I would be seventeen and old enough to drive. I imagined that the young Queen of England would make a special dispensation allowing me (and only me) to drive when I was eight or nine years old. As it was, I had to be satisfied with being allowed to drive our Willys American Army Jeep the mile of our drive to the main road. I was only allowed to do this when we were going somewhere, petrol being still rationed and scarce. As for driving alone, that was permitted when I was transporting horse manure from the pile behind the stable to Father's vegetable garden. I would load up the small heavy trailer and then drive it cross country, through a small stream and a couple of narrow gateways. I soon learned to back the trailer through the third and last gateway without backing over the cliff, which went down the rocks to the line of the high tide. Loading and unloading the manure was backbreaking work for me at that age but seemed well worthwhile if it meant I could drive at all... at eight or ten years old.

Later, when finally I had a licence (at seventeen), each time I met a tourist car on one of the narrow walled lanes in the mountains, I would unhesitatingly race backwards to the last passing place, even if it was two or three hundred yards back, while the other car would have only had to back a few feet – I had found from experience that tourists were hopeless at reversing and it was much quicker to do it myself.

For many years, that Jeep was our family car and Father even drove it 240 miles all the way to London and back. Nowadays, such a trip would seem trifling, but then the roads were very poor and narrow. One had to drive through every town and its market along the way and besides, the Jeep never could go over 50 mph. Its seats were barely upholstered, the suspension felt as if it was non-existent, and the track rods so worn that the front wheels wobbled ominously. They literally flapped between thirty and forty-five miles an hour. Policemen would stop us to say that our front wheels were falling off. Father would reassure them the wheels were safe enough (road worthiness tests were not yet invented) and we would be dubiously waved on. Nor did the drama end when we reached London. Taxi ranks were often in the middle of wide streets and I was sitting beside Mother as she drove closer and closer to the line of taxis. I told her she was getting too close for safety and she scolded me for distracting her attention as she proceeded to scrape the sides of five of them in a row. Being left hand drive and driving on the left side of the road was certainly a handicap, but all her life, Mother was a better horsewoman than driver. The taxi drivers were distraught and a policeman stopped her. After a long discussion and exchange of addresses, he told Mother to "Carry on regardless, but at least get off my beat". She refused to drive any further saying something about "not being responsible for the behaviour of the Jeep!" I admit that there was so much play in the steering, she was not exaggerating. Father had to come and get it.

Another problem of being left hand drive in England was that it was impossible to make hand signals. Of course the Jeep was not fitted with direction indicators for the field of battle, so Nino had fitted it with little red flaps on each side, carved out of wood, which could be raised to indicate a turn by pulling on a string. That was the job of the passenger and I thoroughly enjoyed the responsibility.

Before I started going away to school in 1951, I was mostly 'home schooled'. Mother gave me endless writing exercises of neat loops and twists in a copybook. She taught me to read, but her spelling was so atrocious that I have maintained the same affliction all my life. I started on Beatrix Potter, then *The Wind in the Willows* and fairy tales such as those by Hans Christian Andersen. She taught me about English history, which she enjoyed enormously and we stuck pictures of knights in armour of different eras and styles on pages for different centuries. She tried to teach me the dates of the Norman Conquest and other great landmarks in history. The lives of the average peasant or even the priest were ignored. 'Life' was defined as a catalogue of catastrophes such as death and destruction (for some) and 'successes', for others who had done the killing, raping and burning. There was no mention of what most of us call 'Life'. She also versed me in the Romantic Poets such as Keats, Wordsworth and Shelley.

When it came to arithmetic, sometimes Father would teach me, showing amazing patience and giving clear, methodical explanations so that even I could grasp long division and multiplication in the end. Usually, though, he was too busy writing and I would go to the house of a retired teacher in a village two miles away. I would walk to the Halt or tiny train stop a mile away and take the train for the next mile. Then I would walk up the steep hill behind the village and sit with a bored old lady who had already seen too many reluctant students in her long career...

Occasionally, Mother would invite boys from the village to tea and to play with me but everything conspired against the success of such attempts at assimilation. We lived in a 'Plâs' or large house and travelled to London regularly. Despite Father's efforts to learn and speak Welsh, he only used it in Church to read the Lesson – and I heard that no one could understand him when he did! These boys were painfully polite and respectful. They spoke with a very different accent to ours. Their horizons were circumscribed by their position in society. Yes, they could theoretically break out and move on, but they would certainly have been the exception, not the rule – there has only been one Lloyd George, the only Prime Minister of Britain whose first language was Welsh and who had hired a young Welsh-speaking secretary to correspond with Welsh Constituents. There were many young Welshmen who escaped the drudgery, danger and low pay of working as miners in South Wales by going to America and starting coalmines in Pennsylvania, hiring Irishmen and Poles to work the Face, while the Welshmen now ran the business.

Yes, there are the poets, theologians and other creative people who broke away, but of the boys with whom I played, they all stayed at home, spoke more and more Welsh and some became Welsh Nationalists, virtually refusing to speak English. This, I discovered years later when I met some 'old friends' in a pub. How humiliating they must have remembered their 'play dates' with me!

Years later, in the early sixties, I worked as a labourer on farms, gravel pits and in forestry (first, to pay for my journey to Iran, then across North Africa). My workmates were kind to me, accepting me for the same muddy boots and thermos of hot tea that they all had, although I was 'apart', with my English accent and my 1931 touring car that I had saved from the scrap heap and almost completely restored (it still needed a windscreen and a bonnet – which I could not yet afford), while they came in 'old bangers' or small new cars bought on the 'never-never'. Sometimes they asked me if I lived in a 'Plâs'; I prevaricated, not at all sure that our chaotic, bohemian house really was a 'Plâs' – so they knew… but they didn't seem to hold it against me and we would meet up in the evenings to play Bingo at a Village Hall.

I was never expected to stay in Wales and if I had, I might have been successful in business and so quickly reviled as part of the 'ruling class'. To this day, I cower in shame at the memory of teasing them about their accents... perhaps enough to foment their Nationalism. As much as Father sought integration in church, he could never be considered a real local. I have a niece who now lives there, whose children went to the local school and speak Welsh. Both she and her husband work locally. They are widely liked and relatively integrated. They live in a small house. The divide is not the chasm I knew as a child. The very fact that our neighbours heard Father speaking on the BBC, set us all apart as foreigners. We did not feel wealthy, but in comparison with our neighbours, we most certainly were. We went to private schools, first my Parents and later the rest of us, travelled extensively and spoke one or more European languages.

We spent some Christmas holidays in London for the social and artistic stimulation it afforded and to be away from the cold and damp of Wales. For some years we rented converted stables in Carlton Mews, just off Trafalgar Square. The ground floor had been coach houses and was now used as garages. Access upstairs for the horses was up a long, gentle ramp and then there was a wide balcony or walkway connecting the different stables above. I remember that the wooden loose-box dividers had been removed but the floor remained paved with small stone blocks draining towards huge floor drains. The bedrooms were up a narrow spiral staircase in the haylofts above and in the coachmen's quarters. This was loft-living in London circa 1950. We were right in the centre of the city and I am sure the rent was paltry. It lit my fire for the day when I would move into lofts (and develop them) in New York City in the 1970s.

Mother used to take me out in the evenings to see the bright lights of Piccadilly Circus. Coming from the velvet black nights of our electricity-free area in North Wales, the cascading, erupting, flashing and bursting, the neon-lined periphery of the Circus was fabulous... it only lacked the clowns and lions of an actual circus.

She took me to Hampton Court, the gigantic palace built by Cardinal Wolsey, starting in 1514. By 1528 Henry VIII had broken with Rome, in part because the Pope refused to countenance his desired divorce of Catherine of Aragon and divested the Church of most of its property, including Wolsey's York Palace and Hampton Court. She told me how her elderly Aunt Isabella (known as Nonina) Howard, who had been granted a 'grace and favour' apartment in the Palace, was still living there at the time. The great honour was bestowed on her when she was widowed at the death of her Diplomat husband, Esme Howard. She had gone to stay with them when he was British Ambassador to Washington. She said it was a shame that she had not arranged for us to visit the old lady, but we really could not just drop in on her. What she did not mention was the primitive living conditions endured by these grand old people – minimal heat and food delivered in a basket on a pulley!

She also took me to matinée concerts at the Wigmore Hall and Royal Albert Hall. The classical music could seem interminable to a small child, but I suppose I learned to sit quietly all the way through.

To get there, we would take a double-decker bus (how I loved riding upstairs, with its superior, lofty perspective) or the Tube. Both had sprung, upholstered seats covered in a heavy patterned material somewhere between velvet and a sisal doormat. Everyone smoked on the upper deck and in the smoking carriages of the Tube, mostly cheap Woodbines, their fingers heavily stained with nicotine. Men and women were pale and gaunt; their hands shook as they took another drag on their fags. Sometimes they would be talking to themselves or even shouting at no one in particular. I remember asking Mother why they acted so strangely, she replied: "It's the Blitz". At that age, I had already heard the word 'Blitz' so much in grown-ups' conversation that I knew exactly what she meant: the 1940-41 intense bombing campaign of London and other major industrial cities by the Germans.

It had left a huge proportion of citizens psychologically scarred for life, just as had happened to the inhabitants of Dresden and many other great flattened centres of population. Traumatic Stress Syndrome had as yet no name, but you can be sure it was prevalent, just as it must have been in the Middle Ages and long before. When we walked in the streets, there were signs of the Blitz everywhere: houses cut in half, so that you could look up to half a bedroom, flowered wallpaper on the walls, a washbasin, ragged curtains flying in the wind, once even a bed teetering on the very brink of the abyss where the floor ended. Other buildings had just disappeared completely, leaving a gaping hole in the ground, a gap in the line of buildings, a missing tooth in a huge metropolitan mouth.

Despite great heroism and extraordinary human kindness between all citizens of every class, many people never did recover from the trauma of the Blitz: the sleepless nights in underground bomb shelters, the double and triple work shifts trying to keep the country going without any young men, digging people and body parts from rubble, cordoning off dangerously damaged buildings, losing one's home, one's place of business. It was not just the soldiers who came out of the War scarred for life, but many citizens too. After the War, Britain was left broke, using 97 per cent of funds from the Marshall Plan to pay off wartime debt to America. The conquered and occupied countries of Europe had not accumulated such debt. War reparations represented only 10 per cent of the cost of the British Occupying Forces in Germany. Britain was broke and remained so throughout my childhood – going from the world's biggest creditor nation to the biggest debtor nation. As the Historian Tony Judt put it: "… post-war Britain would have been familiar to citizens of the Soviet bloc, with its constant queues, ration books and shortages."

* * *

Robert Graves' deaf son Sam took me to see a Mickey Mouse film when I was perhaps five. Father was furious – he was determined to protect us from 'trash' culture and had the reputation of being able to smell a comic book if one entered the house. To him, Walt Disney was the anti-Christ while A.A. Milne came a close second with *Winnie the Pooh*. Sentimentality seemed on a par with murder in his moral code. He would find comics (by their smell, we claimed!) with uncanny speed as soon as they crossed the threshold, and then burn them. Sentimentality was purged from the family with Stalinist efficiency to the extent that, bolstered by the 'grin-and-bear-it' regime of boarding schools, I grew up in the belief that one should not feel emotion. If one did, one should hide the fact like dirty laundry and sex. Emotions are messy. Emotions are sissy. Emotions are feminine. Emotions are illogical. Emotions lead one off the 'right path'... whatever the 'right path' is.

So, buried as these feelings were, I came to confuse emotion with sentimentality, love, romance and sex. I spent years of my childhood and adolescence seeking austerity, pushing myself to withstand discomfort: mountain climbing and sailing were perfect trials of endurance. When I was finally seduced sexually, a major *volte-face* in my outlook was introduced in which I had to readjust my childhood misconceptions about sensuality, love and sex.

Sam pretended not to understand what upset Father about the Disney film and went on being his funny goofy self. He cantered like a frisky horse down the streets of London, with little me in tow, talking incessantly and, being stone deaf, quite unintelligibly, very fast, and very loudly.

Father had sold the film rights to his first (highly success-ful) novel back in the 1930s. Still no film had been made yet and the rights were bought and sold several times until, in the 1950s, Disney Studios purchased them. He went into a deep depression about the fate of the film. Nevertheless, his agent suggested to Disney that the original writer help with the script. Quite unannounced, a large black car (with driver) arrived in Wales, all the way from London. It brought three hot staffers 'whiz kids' from Disney six thousand miles away. Father courteously welcomed them and told Mother there would be company for dinner and asked her to take care of their driver while he gave the Americans glasses of Sherry. Almost at once things went wrong when one of the men enthusiastically grabbed Father by his lapels and said: "But you don't get this story, we'll make it into a comic farce with guys slipping over and falling around... it'll be a real comic wow..." Father made the rounds of his guests once more, this time calmly but firmly removing their scarcely-touched glasses. He said: "And now, gentlemen, you shall leave and never trouble me again with your infantile stupidity." They left into the dark night, the way they had come. Disney gave up on the project and sold it to another studio that finally produced it starring Anthony Quinn. Father was mostly a quiet man, but huge in the indomitably of his forceful deter-mination.

Back then, houses in London were still heated with coal fires in each room. The resultant smog (the capillary action of soot particles attracting the water droplets of natural mist) in winter could be so dense that one could not see one's own feet, but had to slide them along looking for the edge of the pavement. Years later, when I worked briefly in an office in London, it was not much better – taking the bus home in the evening, the driver would sometimes pull to the side of the street and ask for a volunteer to guide him. I often did that job, recalling the very early days of motoring when horseless carriages were obliged by law to be preceded by a man on foot with a red flag. Furthermore, I wore a white handkerchief in the breast pocket of my suit (as was the fashion) and when I got home and took it out, the exposed part would be grey with smoke particles while the hidden part was still white.

To this day, if I smell coal smoke it brings tears of nostalgia to my eyes, but what ravages pollution brought to millions of lungs is frightening – the equivalent of a two or three pack-a-day smoking. Indeed, 'nostalgia' may have been another word for an addiction to coal smoke... since I breathed so much of it. Besides, most people smoked as well. Three of us, among my siblings, were asthmatic, which is hardly surprising. They went on being asthmatic for the rest of their lives, but I was lucky: it disappeared when I was twelve. For the next forty years I believed I had been 'cured' of my asthma by being beaten each time I came in last in the school winter cross-country running races. My lungs would seize up with the icy air – as if filled with cement, and I would have to stop to gasp and vomit. Later a doctor told me that asthma often leaves you at puberty. *Q.E.D.*

Mother, being married to a successful novelist, gave 'brilliant' parties in those upstairs stables, attended by some famous intellectuals of the time. Painters, writers, actors, architects and even a few politicians attended. I remember young Peter Ustinov snogging with a new girlfriend. The architects Max Fry and Jane Drew were always lively additions to any party. Lance Sieveking, an old friend, now with the BBC, was over 6'6" and Mother said he was over-sexed – I treated all very tall men with circumspection for some time after hearing that. I imagine he had made an unwanted pass at Mother. Robert Graves and his wife Beryl never came, because they now lived in Deià, Majorca and certainly would not be in London in the winter. Alan Sillitoe, also lived there and though friends with Graves, had not yet struck up his friendship with Father.

The production team from Ealing Studios (with whom Father had been working on a couple of film scripts) also came to these parties: Monja Danischevsky, T.B. Clarke and Charles Frend, who had all been to Wales to encourage him to actually finish a script. In fact, as far as my young eyes could see, they all got tipsy and acted out hilarious scenes together while crippled with laughter.

To my eyes the best of those parties included charades, with some of the shyer young actors wearing masks we'd received for Christmas. One of these masks resembled my Parents' friend and neighbour in Wales, Bertrand Russell. 'Bertie' raised howls of laughter when worn on the face of a shy young cousin. He was one of four children brought up in European Diplomatic circles, all perfectly quadrilingual.

Father complained that his friend (they had dined together several times at a Copenhagen Pen Club meeting) Evelyn Waugh never came to these parties on the pretence that he was 'too old' – though he was three years younger than Father. Other guests included my godfather, Teddy Wolfe, a Bloomsbury painter – as well as Amabel and Clough Williams-Ellis from Wales. Clough always dressed in long jackets like frock coats, cravats and breeches with bright yellow stockings of heavy wool knit. He was an energetic, impetuous man who, well into his nineties, drove much too fast. He once killed a sheep on the mountain road when racing to catch a train. With no shepherd in sight, he pinned his visiting card to the deceased sheep and sped on. Goronwy Rees was another very lively addition. The proceedings were uproarious, but were they brilliant? Or were they just well lubricated with alcohol?

CHAPTER X

DYLAN

Even at my young age, I noticed that one person in particular was never at these parties: *the* Thomas. I was bewildered, because Mother loved to regale guests with tales about Dylan, so I asked her why he was not invited. She brushed off the question by saying that, since the war, his alcoholism had become too much to put up with. Recently, while visiting Laugharne (the model for his most celebrated work: *Under Milk Wood*) in South Wales – where my Parents had lived before the war and been particularly friendly with Dylan, I believe I came nearer to understanding what really happened.

First of all, it seems that Dylan met Caitlin (his future wife) at my Parents' house. They had invited Augustus John and Dylan for the weekend. John arrived in his big car and a date: Caitlin.

After lunch, at which John had noticed how interested Caitlin and Dylan had become in one another, John told Dylan that the two of them were going for a drive. The poet timidly objected, saying he wanted to stay home and write (as in: "Go for a lonely walk with Caitlin".) Well, Dylan was a small man and always broke. John was a big man who drove a big car. That was why he was known by his surname. It was NOT an Optional Invitation. They went for a drive.

Twenty miles away, John stopped the car, leant across his passenger's legs and opened the door for him: "This," he said "is where you get out and walk." Dylan protested, but there was no contest. Dylan went to the nearest pub. He was small and always broke, so people always referred to him by his first name. As it turned out, of course, the scribbler got the girl, while the dauber returned to his perpetual quest for conquests.

Dylan once told an interviewer that he lived in Father's potting shed... poetic licence, for in fact he lived in a pretty little house called 'The Boathouse' a few doors away from my Parents' house – the house with a ruined medieval castle in the garden. Then he and Caitlin moved to a cottage across the estuary, with no telephone and probably no electricity.

Not that all my Parents' hospitality was for intellectuals or the upper class. Father wrote out invitations by hand for every fisherman and cockle man or woman (many of the cockle-pickers were indeed women), inviting them all to dinner at the Castle House.

He later said that a quite remarkable quantity of beer was consumed that night! I remember the piles of empty cockle shells down by the waterfront and the smell was not a savoury one. I came across a jar of preserved cockles in a shop and asked Mother if she liked them. "It all depends where they come from," she replied, reading the label. When she saw they were bottled in Laugharne, she said: "Certainly not! They would leave the fresh cockles out on the dock in the sun for days on end and then wonder why people got sick eating them."

Someone from Laugharne also remarked quite recently, when reminiscing about my Parents: "Mr Hughes would use the Bentley to take children to the hospital in an emergency. He had other cars all right, but the Bentley – that was the quick one. Ran fast indeed it did!"

One morning Dylan appeared at the front door in pyjamas and an old dressing gown. He told Mother that he had come to consult Father on some learned matter... to cross the estuary, he had been rowed by the deaf and dumb ferry boy, dressed as he was for the bedroom. Dylan disappeared into Father's study in a small lookout room in the walls of the medieval castle. Eventually, it was time, and Mother went in to invite Dylan to stay for lunch – the two men were enjoying glasses of dry Amontillado. After lunch (with wine) they retired to their discussion again and soon it was dinnertime. Mother invited Dylan to stay (the two men had moved on to Scotch by then). After dinner, since it was quite clear that Dylan was not going home to his new wife, Mother invited him to stay the night... with the parting thrust of: "At least you will finally be properly dressed for the invitation!" She never forgave him for leaving his young wife with two babies, for more than twenty-four hours, without the possibility of telling her what he was up to – as I've said before, there was no telephone.

The dumb ferry boy, incidentally, was later accused of killing his grandmother, who had been bedridden for so long that she had never seen a car! So it may well have been a mercy killing, but only the family knew what really happened, for it is doubtful that the ferryman had much of a clue about anything. He was a bit simple, besides being deaf and dumb – which had been reason enough not to go to school for a single day. The world around him must have seemed quite incomprehensible. All he understood was the cheerful salutations he received when he went his daily rounds in the village, smiling and waving to people. That was how he got his human feedback. He was acquitted, thanks to a clever young defence lawyer who insisted that a Welsh-speaking deaf and dumb specialist was needed in order to communicate with the accused. When one was finally found, the ferry boy could not understand him at all, having never learned sign language. Could he indeed have understood anything? A mistrial was declared and the poor fellow went back to his work rowing the ferry to and fro. The inhabitants of Laugharne resented any interruption from the outside world. The ferry boy 'meant no harm' – after all, he was always checking in on people and waving to acquaintances across the street – even if he was accused of killing his grandma!

That, at least, was the story I was told. Once again, the story is apocryphal and there have been many more up-to-date versions than those told to me by Father. Even my brother confirmed this version. But in point of fact, it was far more complicated than that. The victim was not his grand-mother, nor was she so ancient and bedridden that "she had never seen a car". It must have been an amalgam of different, disconnected stories, or perhaps just such a murder did occur in Laugharne earlier. Strange things came about in Laugharne all the time.

So indeed, Mother could have felt that Dylan was an enabler to Father, but I believe it went much further than that. Once, when Father was away, he let the poor young poet write in his little study in the lookout room in the castle ruins. Nearby, down a few steps, was the castle dungeon that Father used as a wine cellar. I heard from an old neighbour of my Parents that Father had come back one day to find Dylan in a drunken stupor, surrounded by empty bottles of his best wines. He was not using the study to escape the sound of squalling infants, but to enjoy the cellar nearby. Knowing Father well, I can just picture him taking his small friend (Father being a tall, strong and big man) by the scruff of the neck and walking him slowly off the property, closing and locking the gate without a single word and not once looking back at his brilliant, derelict friend. They never met again, though their mutual respect seems not to have paled.

Well, that is one version of the story, but my oldest siblings assure me that after the war, when Dylan was invited to go on the second (and fatal) lecture tour in America, he came and talked to my Parents about it. On the one hand, with his growing family, he desperately needed the money. On the other, he knew himself too well and had a premonition that he would not be able to resist the temptation of alcohol and its ready availability when he was away from home. What my Parents told him, history does not relate... but of course that was his last trip to America and he died in Saint Vincent's Hospital in Greenwich Village, New York in November 1953.

It seemed to me that everyone in the World was successful, though not necessarily rich, at least in our circles. We were brought up to disdain the rich or at least those who showed their wealth. But it certainly didn't do to be poor either. Then you might have to go out and get a job – that was beneath the ipper class to contemplate! Now, after the war, more and more formerly rich people were indeed having to do just that, but Mother came from a wealthy family. Of course, her great grandfather had made a fortune in the textile industry up North, where the saying goes: '*Where there's muck* [industrial grime], *there's brass* [money]'. He was elected a Liberal Member of Parliament from 1858-80, was knighted on the recommendation of Prime Minister William Gladstone for 'services to the Cotton Industry' – he served on both the Royal Commission for Assimilating Mercantile Law and on both the Great Exhibition of London in 1851 and the Paris International Exhibition of 1855 (receiving the *Légion d'Honneur*). By the time he sold his company in 1861 it was the world's largest manufacturer of fine cotton and lace thread. He bought a vast estate in Gloucestershire with farms and villages on it and moved there – though he never forgot his humble origins and his good fortune. He once wrote in a letter to his son that: "he was not long for this World (actually he lived to 88), that it was his money that had bought his baronetcy and his gentility, but his son should never forget that, for all their huge houses and carriages, they were no better than anyone else". Naturally, his daughter-in-law, Granny Cadogan, was not bound by this credo – she came from a patrician family – and his grandchildren (such as Mother and her siblings) completely forgot his advice and felt they belonged in higher society. It was beneath Mother to open letters from her stockbroker so that, when she died, she still had the same shares in American railroads that she had received when she got married in 1932... which, upon her death, were worthless. I am sure that her grandfather would have turned in his grave had he heard of such lack of husbandry on the part of an heir to the fruits of his labours. After all, he was a highly successful businessman.

Mother's mother, my Granny (his grand-daughter-in-law), was furious when Mother's elder sister married a banker – (as mentioned before, she had referred to him as: 'that counter jumper') for it was beneath the 'upper class' to actually have a job and earn their living... but who bailed out Granny in her old age? Who else but the distinguished banker (the counter-jumper), of course. Meanwhile, Mother's method of spending less was to wander round the house singing: "There's no more money in the bank, oh there's no more money in the bank..." I don't know what we were supposed to do about it, there were no shops in which to spend money, save once a week when we used our petrol rations to go and buy a few essentials, such as kerosene (paraffin to us). If you asked for something in particular at the ironmonger's shop, the invariable response was: "Oh no, such a thing doesn't exist." True, in post-war Britain supplies were very short, but it was quite clear that the Ironmonger's horizon stopped abruptly at their occasional travelling sales-men. Otherwise, we walked a mile each way to the village shop for bread and other such simple essentials, or two miles to the Post Office. We had a new-fangled rucksack with a frame from Norway or a huge basket (said to be from Switzerland) with shoulder straps for carrying baguettes... not that there was anything as fancy as a baguette in Wales.

The only person in the house who always had some cash in his pockets was Father, but Mother paid for our education and the household expenses by cheque. When the local Bank Manager finally saw her coming into the branch for once, he hurried round the counter to corner her:

"Mrs Hughes, Mrs Hughes, it is many the letter I am

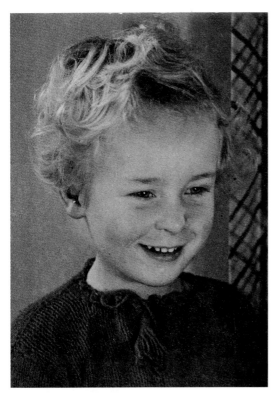

The author aged 3 *left*;
and with faithful dog,
Iago, *below*

Above, Richard Hughes at the centre of an extended family group on his 75th birthday, in the garden of Môr Edrin, the post-war family home of Owain's childhood. And the Hughes family takes tea. Richard Hughes is at the head of the table with Frances Bazely seated to his right. Owain is half way down on the left next to Miss Plimsole.

Facing page: On the estuary. Owain steadies the boat containing his cousins Edward, Henry (at the oars) and Charles Bennett, *top,* and supervises a nautical wheelbarrow of cousins, *middle. Bottom,* Owain with cousins Victoria and Henry Bennett.

Parc, the pre-war family home in north Wales, *top*; the gatehouse of Laugharne castle, *centre*; the beloved Bentley, now restored, *bottom*.

writing to you, indeed, asking what you plan to do about your overdraft… and it's not a single answer that you vouchsafe me. What are you going to do about it, Mrs Hughes?"

"Why Mr Jones, if I only knew what to do, I would have surely answered you, wouldn't I?" That flummoxed the poor man!

While on the forbidden subject of money, Mother kept telling me that "When I came of age" I would "Come into money". That sounded nice, if a little confusing, since she didn't seem to have any left. She assured me that it had been put in Trust for me. Unwisely, I once asked her how much it was, to which she retorted: "It's rude to talk about money and anyway, I don't know. Don't talk about it." Fine, so I shut up, but when I turned twenty one, I was indeed given a check and told to spend it wisely, not fritter it away. It was £135, which was very nice to have, though it paled beside what I had already made from publishing a couple of novels… I had simply no idea what to expect from 'coming into money'!

So my childhood was one of extraordinary privilege in which emotions were not encouraged, founded on the false premise that we were 'upper class' despite having no money – because we had a decrepit old car and never any cash around. In point of fact, my bohemian Parents (who had known many of the Bloomsbury Group) lived very much as they wanted. We had a large house, the grownups drank decent wine, we five children went to private schools (though two won scholarships) and our Parents travelled a great deal. It all made me want to earn a good living and be involved with the 'unsavoury' world of business, with its reality of profit and loss, gross and net earnings. I wanted to travel the world and to have enough money when I did so, to buy myself a drink instead of relying on polluted water.

Which brings me to ice cream: being without electricity, of course we had no refrigerator, save a pre-war kerosene one that worked only very rarely. Even then, sugar was rationed, so the nearest thing I had to ice cream was occasional plain milk frozen in the ice tray. When I was finally treated to a store-bought ice cream, I was already seven or eight and guessed how foolish it would be to bite off the bottom of the cone… but I did it anyway.

XI

BACK TO W.W.II

Like the ubiquitous mosquito, that thrives in the Arctic, the Antarctic and almost everywhere in between from the Amazon to most of Africa and Asia, mankind is almost infinitely adaptable to his environment. When I think what pre-war Wales must have been like for Mother, brought up as she was in a huge house, knowing only the name of the Head Gardener (and of course the same applied for the Head Coachmen, the Housekeeper and the Butler) she never got to know the under-gardeners, kitchen maids, nurses, valets and chambermaids. Now, without servants, she had to face her own arduous destiny single-handedly.

At the outset of war, when Hitler was fully expected to invade Britain at any moment, my Parents were living in a romantic sixteenth-century house high up on the flank of Cnicht in Snowdonia. It was a fine old stone farm manor-house, unchanged in the last couple of centuries: without running water, drains or electricity. The walls were six to twelve feet thick. The thicker walls accommodated a couple of 'priest holes' or early safes. It was always cold and damp. Indeed, it was so damp that soft, velvety emerald green moss grew on the risers of the stairs – even during the driest of months. There she was, with three young children and no domestic help. One day Father announced that he had to go down to the train station to help with the triage of evacuee children from Birkenhead, Liverpool and Manchester. At the end of day, he returned, driving his two-seater Bentley, with a dozen of the least physically or mentally fit children. They had all been refused by local farmers, who were hoping to use them as free labour on their farms. Mind you, the billeting of these evacuee children was not exactly expedited by the fact that the list of possible billeting addresses dated from the First World War, over twenty years before! Not that that was surprising for, as Father wrote after the War, in his arcane history of the British Admiralty: "Much of the shipbuilding machinery in the Tyneside Shipyards dated from a hundred years before!" A point contested by a gentleman who actually read it and declared that "the oldest steam winch was only ninety-eight years old at the time!"

Mother was then saddled with not three, but fifteen children! The newcomers had never walked on grass before, nor eaten a lettuce salad and here they were, swathed in cloud half the time, not an inhabited house in sight, homesick and very unhappy. She did what she could, but was constantly frustrated. The lack of running water came as no surprise to most of the children – in the city they had to get water from a pump at the end of the street, while here the spring was only a dozen yards in front of the door – but there were many other culture-shocks. When offered salad, they said it was rabbit food (many people in cities raised rabbits for food). Once, when Father saw a teenage girl carefully bringing in a huge amount of food in a great Chinese bowl, very likely Ming, he said, "Oh Emily, you really shouldn't be carrying that bowl" – and at that she stopped, opened both her mouth and her hands, and let it smash to smithereens on the slate floor.

My brother remembers being bathed in a tin hip-bath in front of the roaring kitchen fire (on which all the cooking was done) and finding the side away from the fire was freezing cold, while the side near it was scalding hot. Presumably, all the children went through that hip bath and the water cannot have been changed often, given that it had to be brought in from the spring in buckets and heated in the huge kettle that hung on a chain over the fire. What a contrast to having the children brought down, tidily dressed and coiffed at teatime, to be 'seen but not heard'! If Mother had had a nervous breakdown at that point, she would have been fully justified, but instead she soldiered on, 'muddling through' and saved her breakdowns for less inconvenient times, when there were fewer tender souls relying on her.

Fortunately, this early evacuation wave was relatively short-lived. Once the Civil Defence Department determined that there was no immediate danger of invasion and that German bombers would not yet reach so far north, the children could go home again. It was established that the early Luftwaffe was busy enough bombing London, Birmingham, Bristol and literally flattening Coventry. Only later did their range increase and they come further North to Liverpool and Birkenhead. A few of the older evacuees even stayed on in the valley and may still be there, or buried nearby.

Certainly, caring for refugee children was a far cry from Mother's youth. When she was teaching me to ride horses, she told me that as a teenager, her mother insisted she ride side-saddle when she 'rode to hounds' or went fox-hunting. Side-saddle, as required for society ladies, was suicide if you 'rode hard', jumping hedges, banks and ditches along the way, as did she. There is no way to hold on with your knees, save the small pommel of the side-saddle. You stayed on the horse by balance alone. So she used to make arrangements with one of the young stable boys (certainly not the Head Coachman, he was far too faithful to her mother) to bring a normal saddle to a *rendezvous* beyond the end of the drive-way. She would ride out side-saddle to show her mother, then slip to the ground and change saddles as soon as she was out of sight, get a leg-up from the stable boy, tuck in her volumi-nous skirts so as to sit astride and be off to the Meet. Once the hounds were on a scent, she would be up there with the

Master of the Hounds (or rather just behind him, it didn't do to overtake the Master), riding and jumping hell-for-leather. It was a tribute to the landed gentry who rode along behind, that no one mentioned Mother's tricks to her mother! They must have had considerable respect for her daredevil horsemanship, riding as she did like a dashing young fellow.

Now, transplant that rich, spoiled, wilful young lady to the gaunt cold of a stone house in the mountains of Wales, without nursemaid, housemaid, chambermaid or anyone else to do her bidding, save perhaps, briefly and ineffectually, the older Evacuee Children. Totally unaccustomed and unprepared, she rolled up her sleeves, tucked her skirts in her knickers and scrubbed the floors, cooked for a small army and washed and suckled her babies.

Of course, all this was before I was so much as a twinkle in my Parents' eyes, but hearsay and family legend was an integral part of the lore of our existence, just as much as the dog in front of the fire during our story-telling sessions. We collected tales and retold them to such an extent, that Father claimed he could be the origin of a story, but by the time it had made the rounds of his substantial family, it was so totally unrecognizable that he might try telling it himself, only to be scolded by one of his children for misrepresenting the 'facts'... small wonder I had so much trouble with single-word tests at school. 'Facts'? What are these things called 'Facts'?

Father himself gave lectures at the Gresham College in London, in one of which he argued (with considerable logic) that 'fiction' was much nearer the 'truth' than 'non-fiction'. Indeed Gore Vidal also subscribed to the same idea, when justifying his own historical novels. I myself have subscribed to the idea ever since. Anyone who accuses me of skirting the facts, neglects that I am just trying to get nearer The Truth.

XII

HAVEN WITH A SPY

After the untenable fiasco in the bleak mountains of Wales with the poor refugee children, Mother moved back to Gloucestershire, to a house called Barrow Elm, on her brother's estate. There she lived with three, then four and five children as she shared the house with Peter Ustinov's parents, Nadia Benois (the painter) and, with his own tales, Klop Ustinov. Klop was engaged as a spy to befriend suspicious foreigners in London, take them home for the weekend, ply them with good food and drink and see what he could get out of them, frequently speaking their own language (he was fluent in Russian, German, French and of course, English. This resulted in many hilarious stories that he surely embellished, as did his son.

Nowadays, more is known of Klop (his chosen nickname: 'bedbug' in Russian). Born in Palestine in 1891, his grandmother was an Ethiopian Jew. He served in the Luftwaffe during the First World War, but once Nazism took over, his days in Germany were numbered. He held out as a journalist in Germany as long as possible, because he was already working for MI5 as a spy. Finally, he and his wife escaped to England where he secretly introduced important Germans to British politicians in the hope of galvanizing Chamberlain into an aggressive stance on Hitler. To no avail.

Anyway, at Barrow Elm they had running water and drains, with perhaps even a little help from a village girl, when she could spare the time. Everyone pitched in and worked long hours for little or no pay during those intense years of wartime. In an effort to make food less boring, they exchanged recipes that used the few available ingredients. I imagine that Klop Ustinov's wartime job carried a few perks, since he had to entertain his suspects at home... but who knows? Free whiskey was no good for feeding babies!

One of these tales, recounted by Mother (and since she was living with them at the time, she was getting the stories 'hot off the press'), told of Klop escorting one of his Russian 'customers' to the train station in London on a Friday evening to come and stay for a weekend in the country. Klop was an inspired cook and during the week he had scrounged the makings of a lobster thermidor soup. No doubt with food war, it was already remarkable that he managed to obtain any lobster at all, but there would not have been enough to serve half a lobster each, so he had invented a thermidor soup, complete with cognac, cream and cheese. He had placed the soup in a leaky jar and then put it in a hatbox for transport. In the heat of the moment, as he escorted his suspect guest to their first class compartment, he forgot which way up the hatbox was supposed to go. He placed it on the overhead luggage rack, the guest sat below it and Klop sat facing him to engage him in amusing conversation – but he was horrified to see soup dripping out of the hatbox onto his guest's Homburg hat! History does not relate what they had for dinner instead.

Meanwhile, Father had sought mobilization in the army, because he felt guilty at not having served in the First World War, from which whole school classes from the years ahead of him never came back. Robert Graves was one exception who luckily survived. Though five years his senior, he too had been to Charterhouse School (five years ahead of Father) and was first reported 'missing in action' then, 'killed in action'. Finally, he was brought back to Britain on a stretcher with only half a lung left, to find accolades in his newspaper obituaries, speaking of the waste of losing such a young talent. Father said that Graves became impossibly arrogant and conceited at that time... but that had worn off by the time I met him. The last time I saw him, he was in his seventies and he out-walked me across Oxford, having developed his half lung to the size of two by sheer willpower and strenuous exercise. He died at ninety.

At 39, Father was deemed too old for action, so he was found a desk job at the Admiralty in London and worked as a fire warden by night. Like many of his contemporaries, after the war, he found it difficult to readjust to peacetime. Once installed in our house on the estuary in North Wales, not only did he wire it for electricity (the 12 volt windmill), but gardened hard, raising vegetables and fruit besides setting two varieties of fish net and night lines to catch fish on the rising tides. He was often down on the sand flats at low tide, cleaning and mending his nets, baiting the nightlines. Sometimes he would catch a nice bass, but most of the time it was plaice (that poor cousin of the Dover sole – I always thought they tasted of the mud in which they lived and fed.)

Grass could grow in the shallow earth that covered the shale, here and there a stunted tree or two, but for a vegetable garden you needed compost and manure. He worked on the quality of the earth for years using horse manure with its bedding straw and seaweed from the beach. He managed to produce many of the things that were unobtainable in the shops, either because of rationing, or because no one produced them and no one asked for them: sweet corn, asparagus, Cos (Romaine) lettuce, beans, peas, artichokes, rhubarb and strawberries.

When he tried to grow berries, the birds immediately devoured them – after all, this was the only fruit garden within many miles. He built a huge wire-mesh cage to keep the birds out and inside produced raspberries, black and red currants and gooseberries. From these fruits, Mother canned and jarred quantities of jams, but since sugar was so severely rationed, it never set and quickly went mouldy. We found them delicious and even claimed to feel a little kick from the fermented fruit.

All of this providing of food cut into his writing day and for the rest of his life he had great trouble finishing anything. He shot rabbits and wild duck. Cartridges for the 12-bore shotguns or the .22 Winchester were expensive and only to be used for bringing home food. Target practice was not allowed, you cannot eat a tin can if you shoot it, but you just might bag that wild duck.

It was my job to burn the waste paper and cardboard down at the high water mark, so I witnessed the vast quantities of his discarded typescripts. The flames would lick hungrily through the painstakingly-filled pages. He would retype each page up to forty times each time it became illegible from his tiny, densely hand-written changes. He once said that his best editor was his bank manager. Once his overdraft hit rock bottom and could go no further, he was forced to send off his current typescript.

The war over, Mother had gone back to painting. Earlier, she had painted landscapes and individual trees. She had an especially sensuous relationship with trees and loved to paint their limbs, as they grew out from their trunks. She told me how, as a little girl, she would climb huge old trees in the park of their home, sit astride great boughs in her long white pantaloons, her white skirts tumbling torn and dirty around her, and piss on the branch, for the sheer sexual pleasure it gave her. Now she turned to the hills and rugged mountains she could see from her studio, painting them in different lights and cloud cover, with and without snow caps. Modestly, she never signed a painting, nor did she ever sell one for her own profit. It was always for some charity or other, usually the Red Cross. Once, as she sat on the low wall of the terrace on the North side of the house sketching the mountains, I asked her why she only painted mountains, never people. I quickly saw why. She rapidly did a sketch of me that showed such utter impatience with human beings, I never asked again.

Later, when I was away at boarding school, she took to going on little trips by herself. By then she had bought a small second-hand 1948 four-seated Hillman convertible. She would set off with her painting materials, a sleeping bag, tent and billycans. Sometimes she would sit in the car to paint mountain ranges, holding her palette and brushes in her left hand and propping the small canvass or sketchbook on the steering wheel. The result, of course, was that the convertible top of one car after another was slashed with strokes of oil paint above the driver's seat.

She told me that, as a young woman, she had been a scout master and taught little village boys how to make a fire in the rain, how to scour pots and pans with the earth and gravel found under a tuft of grass (which served as handle for the scourer), and set up a drying rack made of sticks stuck in the ground for drying them. She taught my youngest sister and me these skills too and I must have been eight or nine when the two of us set off on ponies, with tents, and then rendezvoused with Mother sixty hours later, on the far side of the Snowdonia mountains.

When she went off alone, she would just ask a farmer if she might pitch her tent in the corner of a field (without cows – they become inquisitive and tend to want to join one in bed.) No farmer refused this middle-aged lady with windblown hair. Indeed, they would often come down later to see if she had everything she needed and were duly impressed by her camping skills. She continued in these excursions until she was seventy, by which time her arthritis refused to let her sleep on the ground any more. By then she was painting waterfalls, often clambering down the sides of gorges and sitting in the spray from a cascade. She seized the movement of water with a few quick strokes of her brush, giving the impression of a Japanese sketch.

She also used her little car to bring home bales of hay for

the horses, piling them on the open trunk lid and up over the rear window. Inevitably hayseeds fell into the rubber seal around the glass window and with a little rain, they sprouted in a trim fringe of very green grass... I once saw Father carefully clipping this grass with his best beard-cutting scissors – saying he was just giving it a hair cut "so that Mother can safely see out of the back window". A sense of the surreal was happily shared by both of them, though their blazing rows intimidated me and to this day I cannot stand altercations. Anyway, she never looked in her rear-view mirror – the unfolding developments ahead were always more than enough to take her full attention. Horses do not have rear-view mirrors, so why should these horseless carriages or motor cars?

XIII

RAIN, SEX, SCHOOL

Endless rainy days, before I could read, brought marathon introspection and self- exploration. Sex and sexuality were, of course, black magic mysteries to me. With no television to give me examples of 'standard' behaviour, my imagination ran amok like a snipe that breaks cover with wild, rapid zigzags up into the sky to confuse its hunters. Of course I had no concept of what sex was for, but I was acutely aware that certain images and sensations aroused me in a pleasant way. I don't know when I learned to read, but I was a late starter. Certainly I could read and write by the time I was sent away to school at seven, so this period was probably when I was four or five.

Someone had read to me from an illustrated children's book about a hare. I remember a feminine voice reading that the hare was a 'scamp'. I forget why. But somehow the word 'scamp' took on a sexual connotation in my mind. There was something erotic in the stance of the hare on its hind legs, with its slim waist and powerful furry thighs that obsessed me. I was terrified that Father would find the book, deem it 'sentimental', and banish it forever. So I hid it carefully and only took it out to lust over the illustrations when I was safely alone… it might as well have been a copy of *Playboy* or *Hustler*.

Another obsession was my underwear. I suppose that all boys of my age at that time were condemned to wear thick woollen underpants that were extraordinarily scratchy. As a teenager, I had to join the school Officers' Training Corps for which we carried World War I .303 Lee Enfield rifles (stamped with their dates of manufacture: 1917 or 1918). Mine had corrected sights and was amazingly accurate for such a hated and abused old piece of steel and wood. But it was the uniforms that I really hated: the material was so scratchy it felt as if it had been made of Brillo pads cut in half. Also, when wet, it stank, not just of wet dog, but of wet and miserable Army Issue. Fatigues were of heavy cotton and vastly preferable for their texture, even if the tasks we performed in them were worse than all the rest. So I preferred to dig trenches in the pouring rain, but in my fatigues, than to stand to attention on the parade ground on a summer's day, in my scratchy uniform.

Now, had there been long silk underwear at the time, I would surely have been less miserable in the OTC. Well, at this tender age, I discovered a pair of underpants, full of holes, that may well have belonged to a female relative (I know my sisters had to wear navy blue knickers that were not much more sensuous than my own, so they were not theirs). Since Mother had already shown me the rudiments of sewing, I clumsily repaired the holes and wore them to the exclusion of my 'official issue' underwear. Made of brushed cotton or perhaps a silk/cotton blend their softness was a sexual caress. When no one else was taking any interest in my solitude and rain precluded the great outdoors, I would go to bed in my underpants and look at the hare book and squirm with mysterious pleasure. Even the word 'pants' (underpants in English) or 'shorts' (as in American underpants) held a sexual connotation for me. For me shorts were shorts and trousers were trousers or even 'bags'. Pants were underpants.

I also discovered, in the paint and tool shed, an enormously thick copy of *Vogue* magazine from the forties. While *Vogue* was careful at the time not to run advertisements for corsets and foundations, considering them far too vulgar, there were so many references to femininity in the pictures... while at the same time *Harper's Bazaar*, besides publishing good short stories and articles by Hemingway, Faulkner and even Father, did not have such scruples and since the edition with Father's article in it was in the house, it eventually became my version of *Playboy* or *Penthouse*, thanks to its advertisements for foundations, *guèpieres* and lingerie.

★ ★ ★

I was still seven years old when Mother took me to the station and put me on a train to London. It was an eight-hour journey and involved changing trains twice, once in Welshpool and once again in Shrewsbury. Things were different in those days and she asked the guard of the train to look out for me and make sure I made the first change of trains.

After that, he probably asked another passenger to hand me on in Welshpool to the next guard, through to Shrewsbury where the process would be repeated when I was handed on to the London train. I have no recollection of how much grownups helped or ignored me. As far as I was concerned, I just carried on. In retrospect, I am sure that many a kind adult assisted me. Mother and I had already travelled by train to London a few times, but it was less stressful traveling alone than with Mother: she always had so many packages that, like a flock of sheep, she had to keep counting them, to make sure she hadn't left one behind. I just had one very large suitcase, which I am quite sure was too large for me to handle, so someone must have been helping me along the way... so no doubt I just followed my suitcase. Mind you, her parting words to me were: "Now, do not speak to strangers...". Just how does a seven-year-old child travel from North Wales to London by train, changing trains twice and taking a taxi in London, manage without talking to helpful strangers and accepting their assistance? Even at twice the age, travelling by three ferries and four trains from the Dodecanese Islands in Greece, home, I was 'kidnapped' by some older teenage

French girls and had a night's sleep in a real bed in Paris!

Once in London, I took one of the quaint old nineteen forties London taxis that could turn in little more than their own length. I gave the driver the address of Nan, a friend of Mother's – she was divorced from the Liberal Member of Parliament, Wilfred Roberts (he was already out of the picture by then) and she lived in a large elegant house in a splendid walled garden across the road from Hampstead Heath. Nan tried to persuade Mother to buy paintings by Mondrian (which were selling for a pittance at the time) but she replied that, though she liked his early flowers and trees, she could not accept his later geometric work… just what thrilled Nan so much. When I arrived, I paid my fare and (following instructions) offered the driver a tip. But he waved it aside with: "No, no, sonny, you'll be wanting that soon enough for a cup of hot tea".

That first year I went to a day school called Byron House in Highgate with Judy, daughter of another family friend. I lodged at their house, up the street from Nan's house on Keats Grove and right opposite the Romantic poet's own house. The houses on that street were elegant Queen Anne, all set back in their own gardens – though none as large as Nan's. Father's literary agent (David Higham) had a lovely house between the two friends.

Mother had seen Judy and her mother, Jess, camping in a field near our house in Wales. The weather was dreadful and for days the dreary rain would not let up, so she invited them over to dry out their clothes in the kitchen and play with us indoors. They soon became good friends and continued to be so, long after I stayed with them.

Jess was a staunch Socialist – a neat trick for someone who owned such a lovely house and lived off the proceeds of stock in Cadbury's chocolate. The Cadburys were Quakers and lived unostentatiously, giving lavishly to many charities. But Jess did not believe in God or Church and discouraged any vague interest I might have shown. However, Father's godfather (he looked like G.B. Shaw, with his spare frame and great white beard) lived at the top of Keats Grove and sometimes took me to the pretty church at that end of the street. It was something one did. He lived happily with his younger (second) wife, taking her breakfast in bed every day in their bedroom upstairs. I picture him walking up the stairs with a tea-tray loaded with breakfast accoutrements. Methodical, precise and gallant. In conversation with Mother one day, he said: "I believe it was a mistake to live over 90."

"But why Charles? You seem so happy!"

"Well, my dear, one begins to feel... how should I put it? Perhaps a little 'middle-aged'? Trouble lacing ones shoes and such...". He was 96 and died peacefully later that year.

Besides the godfather, there was also a summer neighbour from North Wales (a German Jewish refugee from Nazi Germany before the war). He too lived at the top of the street. That made five different friends of my Parents all within one hundred yards of each other, in the elegant neighbourhood of North London: Hampstead.

The walk to and from school seemed interminable. There were few distractions along the way, so I would think of Father's tales of walking to school. There was the time he met a baby bird on the ground on his way to kindergarten: he chatted with it for a while and then carried on to school, only to find that the other children were already leaving as he arrived! Such is time to a very young child. Then there was the time that he fell in love with an older girl and could not bear to walk into the classroom with her eyes upon him, so he made his entrance with a series of summersaults. Her reaction was to scold him with: "Get up off the floor, don't you see you're getting your clothes dirty?" The spell was broken and he was out of love in a trice.

When the first snow fell, a friend of Judy's invited us to go home across Hampstead Heath and try out her new skis with her. My introduction to the sport was as patchy as the melting snow, but I do remember a few thrilling slides and less thrilling falls. By the time we reached home, Jess had called the police and reported us missing, but fortunately for me, Judy was a year or two older than I, so she was the scapegoat and took the brunt of the blame.

Another time, we were walking on the Heath together when a man came up to me with a persuasive invitation to see something very special that he was sure I had never seen before. He was right. But what is so special about watching someone else jerk off? Ever since, I've always felt it is something to be enjoyed oneself – not exactly a spectator sport. I think I can still remember the man's dirty old raincoat, frayed scarf and nicotine-tainted breath, but those memories are vague and may well have come from later indoctrination – they seem too typical. Perhaps he was a well-dressed, good-looking young man, but that was not the memory I have of him. Judy discovered us behind the bushes and said it was time to go home for tea... now I am sorry I did not thank her for that intervention. Fifty years later, when she joined me for lunch at my photo studios in New York, I could have done just that. I could have thanked her. I regret the omission. She might well have forgotten the incident, or had some other slant upon it, but I didn't even mention it. Another missed opportunity, that might have revealed that she saw nothing of my experience, or there again, she might have felt she was saving me from embarrassment and perversion. After all, I had been precociously enjoying myself ever since 'Benty' was towed away, though we all know that sex comes with few, if any, users' manuals.

At all events, London was a far cry from my solitary existence in Wales, in the rain, without electricity or playmates... I had stimulation from the current world, instead of being isolated at home in North Wales.

XIV

MISTY MOUNTAIN

The next year, I went to a weekly boarding school in the opposite direction, walking back to Judy's home for weekends. It was housed in red brick Victorian buildings amongst quiet streets of substantial, elegant townhouses. The assembly hall (or was it the chapel?) and classrooms were on the lower floors and dormitories for the ten per cent of weekly boarders were up in the attics, right under the beams and trusses of the roof.

I remember the intense bewilderment of that first day at school with no one to point me in any particular direction. Everyone seemed to know what they were doing and where they were supposed to be, except for me. Eventually I went into an empty classroom and sat down. Some time later, a class came crashing and shouting in and sat down, ignoring me. When the master arrived to subdue the rabble, he spotted me at the back and asked me what I thought I was doing. Truthfully I said I did not know. I had no 'thought', I had no 'plan', I was simply trying to be out of the way. Now I know to temper the truth – it can so easily be misconstrued.

With threats of a beating, I was taken to the correct class-room, already labelled as a devious, lazy smart aleck. Very soon I was known as Misty Mountain and drifted cluelessly through my classes, school prayers and football (soccer), rugby, boxing and cricket. In my bewilderment, I took refuge in my misty mountain disguise. Foggy detachment stayed with me and most of the classes floated over my head like the motes in sunbeams that fascinated me so much more than did lessons. Boxing was purgatory. We boxed in stockinged feet on a parquet floor, to teach us balance – every other boy was faster than I was so I served as a punching bag, trying desperately not to lose my slippery footing on the polished floor. Boxing was to make men of us. Doing it in socks on a slippery floor was supposed to give us balance and poise. Instead it gave me a life-long aversion to fisticuffs.

We sang that jingoistic anthem 'Rule Britannia' as well as the National Anthem: 'God Save the King' (soon to become: 'the Queen') at every excuse possible – I was too young to see the absurdity in lauding a country that was broke from fighting the War, miserable from rationing and shortages, standing in queues, struggling to 'make do'. Britain was certainly not 'broken', given its straightened circumstances, it was still remarkably cheerful and brave, but as for 'ruling the waves', the concept was ridiculous. Old habits die hard and in those days, everyone stood to attention for the National Anthem before every film or concert started. The stiff upper-lip and 'carry on regardless' attitude held people together. After all, the whole of Europe was flat broke after the war, at least Britain had 'won' the war, but what was left of the British Empire? The very fact that Britain stubbornly tried to go on 'ruling the waves' with its naval fleets and RAF squadrons and soldiers stationed in foreign countries, was exacerbating its gloomy economic situation. The brave bluster (and sometimes incredible stupidity and narrow-mindedness) of the Charge of Light Brigade, in which almost an entire cavalry brigade was decimated by Russian troops near Sebastopol, thanks to rigid training, squabbling officers and muddled miscommunication, carried on. How I remember the news arriving at school that Colonel Nasser was nationalizing the Suez Canal, creating an international crisis. A very fat old master cried out (his face apoplectic with enthusiasm): "Hoorah! Let's send in the battleships… that'll teach those Wogs a lesson!"

To quote the Communist Djilas (oh how my school masters would turn in their graves!): "The manipulation of fervour is the germ of bondage." So the 'servant class' (or what remained of it after the war) still seemed proud of the expensive habits of their bosses. They did not seem to aspire to anything much better. Thanks to unions and several left wing governments, the playing field has been levelled a great deal since then and everyone can at least aspire, even if higher goals are not really attainable. These were the dying gasps of the British Empire.

The one event, upon which I could count every evening, was the arrival of the 'Head Man' to say "goodnight" to us in our dormitories under the rafters. He was a spare, grey-haired man who had taught for many years in the British Raj in India, that behemoth of the then so recent past. Here he was back in England with his mementoes of the East: an elephant's foot made into a stool, ivory knickknacks, rugs and so forth. Every night he would come to our dormitory under the roof of the school and say: "Lights out now. No talking in bed and... Hughes, in the bathroom!" and there he would whip me with what looked like an elephant's tail. He told me to take down my pyjama trousers and then he would bend me over the side of the great claw-foot bathtub in which we all shared the water on our bath nights. I suppose he inflicted physical pain on me, but I forget. What I do know is that I never understood why I was being punished. It was just something that happened every night.

I did once mention these nightly chastisements to my Parents and I think they were slightly embarrassed. Father said nothing beyond asking what I had done – a question I was utterly unable to answer. Mother said something about "That is how schools are run." Certainly, if corporal chastisement was what they were paying for, in me they got their money's worth! By the time I came along, physical punishment seemed to be too distasteful for them to carry out themselves. Even physical contact, such as hugs and kisses fell to taboo. How I later envied French children who kissed formally several times a day and would walk from one room to another with an arm around a Parent – or vice versa.

Our dormitory was on the top floor of the school, under the roof. Instead of tie-beams to prevent the rafters from spreading, there were huge iron rods with threaded ends that held the roof together. These horizontal rods were perhaps eight feet above the floor, but easily accessible to small boys, jumping up from the height of their beds. We could then perform all sorts of gymnastics on these bars, but the favourite was simply to swing Tarzan-style and leap onto one's neighbour's bed. No doubt producing a resounding thump in the process, which would echo in the empty class-rooms below. I particularly remember a boy called Ralph, who once managed to leap beyond his neighbour's bed and almost made it to the next one over, but crashed painfully and ignominiously to the floor instead. Ralph did not try that again.

Dormitories in these schools were unheated (as were the classrooms) and the carafe of drinking water provided for us would have a skin of ice on it when we awoke in the pitch dark of winter mornings, to get up and hurry off to class.

Even at my next school (this one, in a huge Georgian mansion on a hill, far out in the countryside) where a differ-ent punishment continued relentlessly, I never understood for what I was being punished. This headmaster had decided that I needed a two-hour lecture every Saturday afternoon. I have no idea what he was talking about to me, all alone. Sometimes I just wished he would flog me like the other boys and get it over and not take up my precious time by rambling on and on. Now I wonder about his own precious time… Why was I punished? Probably just for being me – though murderers don't get away with that excuse either. To add to my bewilder-ment, at this, my third school, I was also the headmaster's 'pet', often taken with him in his car on errands, then lectured into oblivion every Saturday afternoon. What a waste of a nice Saturday afternoon! I came to think of these punishments as pure bureaucracy, no doubt necessary for the system, but an awful waste of time. Both his, mine and the school's.

Yes, I do confess, that my first day at this third school, I was roundly scolded for apparently taking my time in walking up to the master's desk when summoned. I replied with something to the effect of: "… when you reach my great age and time of life, you'll see…" such facetious 'wit' was not appreciated. I wonder where it came from? I don't believe my Parents were facetious, it was far more likely that it was school-grown and I was just emulating my bored, cynical, dissatisfied teachers. Anyway, I learned to button it up and never again try to make jokes to those in authority. I was clearly a most objectionable brat. Nowadays, it is recognized that I am dyslexic and the learning process something of a complicated mystery to me, but I muddled through, distracted and vague and thank god, no one tries to beat me any more. I wonder if it did me any good or any harm?

An instinct within me (it must have come from my Parents, though I wonder how and why) disdained my teachers. Although they were the holders of the knowledge I was supposed to absorb, I believe I felt superior to them. Once a week we had to write informative letters home and these would be read by the headmaster and given back with corrections, to be recopied, if there were too many mistakes in spelling and grammar. Mother had told me by letter that my Parents might visit me on a weekend not designated as a visiting weekend. As if to tempt the gods, I wrote back that they could probably persuade the Head to let me go out with them, although it was not the correct weekend – this, knowing full well that the Head would read my letter. My motivation is still unclear to me, but I suppose I was testing the waters of authority. Would Father's celebrity carry the day, or would it be the petty authority of the headmaster? Not surprisingly, I was denied the outing with my Parents and I am sure the

Head explained to them exactly why. I had overdone it. I had pushed my luck too far. I had teased the sleeping dog too much and it had bitten me.

As for my teachers, almost all the good ones were homosexuals. While they did not practice what they perhaps desired, their leanings were obvious from the occasional, nonchalant caress, besides the fact that they were often vastly over-qualified for their jobs. They were not pederasts and I never heard of an incident of molestation. Many of them were married, though often without children. As for the mediocre teachers: they were the rule. They were bored, had little control over the boys and sometimes had every lesson (complete with appropriate jokes) in an old binder that had served them for the forty years or so of their careers. To my intense embarrassment, these bad teachers could even be reduced to tears by the nasty herd of children in their care.

My pattern of learning was dictated by an extraordinary lack of memory for anything I was told to learn by rote. As a result, when given a weekly test of twenty questions with one-word answers, I invariably scored only one or two correct answers and would be at the bottom of the class. These positions in the class hierarchy were constantly drummed into us in order to 'encourage competition'. – I have strenuously avoided competition ever since. Yet, given the opportunity to write an essay on some subject, I invariably came in first or second, once being given a score of 110% - just how can you beat 'perfection'? In an essay, I could get around the gaping holes in my factual knowledge and write about cause and effect instead. Quite frequently, my teachers attributed this poor test performance to extreme laziness on my part and concluded that I had not even tried to do my homework or preparation. I could study a poem or a list of dates or names for hours on end, without any of it being committed to my memory... then I would read something that struck me (such as *The Old Man and the Sea*, or Lord Tennyson, Marlowe or Vachel Lindsey) and find I could quote whole pages verbatim after one reading. Of course, these accusations of laziness were often followed by more corporal punishment even though I already spent far more time on homework and preparation than anyone else. When I reached high school (or rather a private school which is called public school in England), I resorted to getting up at three or four in the morning, using a skeleton key to get out of the dormitory wing and go to my study to prepare for the day's classes. Nor did it end when I went home for holidays. My Mother constantly drummed into me how much more brilliant were my older siblings. The eldest two had won scholarships, while I was just barely accepted at every school I attended.

Years later, someone told me that the 'Head Man' (the Indian Raj veteran who beat me every night) at my second school had been E.M. Forster's model for the young English teacher in *A Passage to India*. When I read the book, I could find no resemblance between him and the young, relatively liberal and idealistic schoolteacher of the book. Besides, Forster's character was single and this old man with silver hair, married. I wonder if he had children, and if he did, whether chastising them had satisfied him much – or if perhaps, like many other parents, he farmed them out for corporal punishment.

Of all the years of tedium that I have totally forgotten, there are motes of souvenir that float into my mind from time to time: I do remember my very first French classes, taught by a Frenchman. The first thing we learned being the alphabet in French, a sensible thing to learn that helped me enormously with pronunciation, though we all thought it infantile, we were much too big to be learning the alphabet all over again. I remember making an egg rack in carpentry class, which served my Parents well in the larder for many years thereafter. The French alphabet and an egg rack – were these to be my monument to an expensive private education?

At each of these schools, the National Religion or Church

of England was taught and applied by prayers every morning and then there was always Church on Sundays. I don't think I started reflecting upon religion until I had travelled in lands where other rites were practiced: Catholicism, Greek Orthodoxy and Islam. I just went to Church and made sure I was not perceived as a rebel. I had enough trouble without being seen as a rebel too. I pretended to toe the party line even if I did have the occasional, anarchistic desire to strip naked and run up the nave of the church, leap onto the altar and mimic Christ on the cross, or perhaps sit cross-legged, Buddha-like, on the altar. The consequences would have been grave. Was it that I was looking for the limelight, anonymous student that I was? Did I truly seek to shock? I never ever thought of spraying the congregation with bullets (as has happened all too frequently of late). Quite simply, I had been raised to think of bullets as tools for getting food, besides being used in wars, with such terrible consequences that the idea never crossed my mind. That we had no television, meant I never witnessed the cheapening of human life, by seeing multiple killings on the box before noon – an average of 157 in Japan when I worked there in 1970! As I saw it, the congregation was not food, nor fair game, they were not rabbits, wild duck or even, for that matter, wild boar! Just to shock and surprise these few hundred suited and tied men, young and old, why would I risk my skin?

Of the hundreds of sermons I heard, I do remember one: the preacher told of walking down a fancy street in London and seeing some truly beautiful gardening tools in a shop window. He stepped back and saw that it was the street presence of the venerable Sword Makers – Wilkinson's of London, founded in 1772. Thus he launched into the theme of 'beating swords into ploughshares'. I liked that sermon and have remembered it.

The food in these schools was at least made in the kitchen, there was no packaged food in those days, but in order to make a profit from private schools, a single joint of meat had to be shared by about fifty boys and six or eight staff. It was English food at its most ordinary and tasteless. Still, by then, food could be bought – when my brother was in school during the war, the boys were so hungry that they would share any food from home amongst the whole dormitory. One boy received an enormous Shepherd's Pie. The whole dormitory was treated to one spoonful a night and it was carefully hidden under the bed of the owner. They never dared look at it in daylight or by electricity, lest they be caught – after several days, the entire dormitory was violently sick and told to spend the day in bed. By daylight, they pulled out the meat pie and looked at it – not only was it very furry and green by then – but the boys had been eating spoonfuls of live maggots as well!

My particular pain, my most miserable dressing down, worse by far than any lashing or tongue-lashing inflicted by headmasters, always came when the school matron opened my large suitcase (the other boys had trunks) at the beginning of each term or semester. On the top would be the 'Required Clothing List' of the school. The list had boxes to be crossed off as each required quantity of clothing was packed.

I always packed my own suitcase. I suppose Mother thought that was part of managing on one's own. Or perhaps it was one thing too many for her to cope with. Since I did not have the requisite quantity of each item, I just checked them off and hoped that no one would notice. Those matrons had mostly served as nurses in the armed services during the war. For them regulations were regulations. Be a Man and Die For Your Country – and if you're such a miserable wimp as to just get wounded, the nurses would patch you up and send you back in to try again.

At the beginning of every term, I would be summoned for this tongue-lashing by a huge matron, bursting out of her starched uniform with apoplectic indignation. She would tell me, in no uncertain terms, that if Mother couldn't do better than this, I should be going to a state day school and not expect the great advantages that private school would afford me in my illustrious future. I never confessed that it was I who packed my own bag and that apart from the essentials of school uniform (which had to be purchased in London), nothing much was available in Wales. That my muddy wellington boots were on top of my clean grey flannel shorts without any protective packaging, drove those ladies to despair. Nowadays, I have to understand their dismay.

I did have one pair of boy's underpants that were not made of 'rough grit sandpaper' and I would wear them for the twelve weeks of term time, turning in the scratchy woollen ones as dirty every week. The Matron's tongue-lashing slowly subsided into the general miserable pain, confusion and sorrow of beginning a new term. I doubt I substantially changed my packing techniques, for one thing, I could never have found the requisite wrapping paper. It was kept under the hearth rug of my Father's study and he could never be disturbed while he was working. So I just reefed sail and battened down my emotional hatches for the storm I knew was bound to hit.

We once had a most pretty, even engaging, kind and enchanting young assistant matron. She was a model and happened to be 'resting' from modelling. She told us she had an eighteen inch waist. I am sure I was not the only boy to adore her. And then she was gone. She scarcely lasted a month on the job. She was far too likeable… I shall never forget her. For two-thirds of the year, boys like myself were deprived of female companionship. The women we encountered during term time were either sergeant major battleaxes as matrons or perhaps the stray dried-up, sad ladies who taught advanced Mathematics or Physics. A pretty, flirtatious young woman was a ray of sunshine in the desert of our sexuality.

XV

MOUNTAINS AND GUNS

Outside the school in London, we would go and visit a small toy shop where the owner would sing us dirty songs ("Auld Ma Kelly, with a Bamboo Belly and Her Tits Tied Up With String…") and seemingly overlooked the shop-lifting exploits of my classmates. I never tried theft because I knew it was wrong and above all, I did not want to be caught. I had enough chastisement in school for things I did not comprehend, why look for more? Perhaps the 'Head Man' was whipping me to stop me even thinking of shoplifting. If that was the case, then it certainly worked.

As a teenager, the then Chancellor of the Exchequer – my neighbour at dinner at Pratt's, a very select gentleman's dining club to which Father once took me told me that the purpose of the 'public school system' (private, exclusive schools) was to instil a certain deviousness and a capacity for bending the rules "without ever getting caught." Yet government ministers seem to be getting caught in droves these days. Perhaps the English private school system is no longer doing such a good job… For my own part, by his judgment, I did pretty well. By the time I had finished high school, I had an illicit car kept at school, smoked cigarettes (which I hated, but they were forbidden) and kept a cocktail cabinet inside a large old wireless, whose clumsy valve intestines I had replaced with a transistor set – which left plenty of space for bottles. I also had a girlfriend in a neighbouring boarding school and frequently broke the 30-mile limit for excursions on days off – I was clearly learning 'to get the ropes'. Incidentally, to avoid the problem that gentlemen might encounter when unable to remember the names of the staff at Pratt's, they were all called 'George' – it was considered more friendly than just calling out: "My good man!"

One landmark remains in the blur of those early years: a slideshow given by a member of the Edmund Hillary-Tenzing team that made the first successful ascent of Everest. I am fairly sure that the lecture was not given by Sir Edmund himself, though I did meet him elsewhere. No, I believe it was given by one of the support team who climbed as far as the last base camp… I vividly remember the unreal blue of the Nepalese skies and brilliant white fangs of the Himalayan peaks, of those early Kodachrome slides. My fantasies about becoming a rock climber were never fully realised, though I did climb some tricky crags in Wales, rocks that had claimed more than one life before and after me. I was about to meet my first climbing buddy and I was just nine years old by then.

I remember James Morris, the journalist who cabled news of the success of that ascent, when he came to visit my Parents, as a very manly man – a war hero and invincible journalist who wore heavy tweeds and stout hiking boots. I believe he even smoked a pipe at the time. Now well known as Jan Morris the travel writer, following a sexual realignment procedure, she was visited by Paul Theroux (as described in his book, *The Kingdom by the Sea*) and they compared notes on sexual advantages when packing for a trip. He said Jan had the ultimate authority when she told him: "It's so much easier as a girl, one just shoves a couple of little frocks in a rucksack and off one goes." As Theroux remarked: "… and she must have known about the comparison more than anyone!"

In my dormitory, I met Alan Trist, only son of a social psychologist. His mother had been in a country mental institution since Alan was two years old. There was an 'aunt' who lived with his father and eventually became Alan's stepmother. He had a long, elfin face, narrow, with pointed chin and ears. He was slightly built for his age, but tough – considering that he was a city dweller. As time went on, I often invited him to come and stay with us in North Wales and despite Father's philosophy of 'benign neglect' in raising children, Alan got a lot more attention and company with us than he did at home in London. He was ahead of me in class, so during the school day we had no contact with each other, but at night, after lights out, when we were forbidden to talk, we chatted about this and that… now that I think about it, he never spoke about himself, so I must have done much of the talking myself, no doubt describing (boasting of? Boys do that) life at home.

Eventually, Alan came to stay with us during school holidays until we had accomplished our journey to the Holy Isle of Bardsey. There was a lunch at our great family table. It was full with fourteen people. Alan was feeling brave and started regaling all present with his escapades around home in North London – thank God he did not mention the air gun battles! He was telling us how he and another friend used to enjoy climbing a huge wall around a great garden, where there were magnificent apple trees, laden with fruit. They would pocket as many as possible, until the vicious old lady homeowner set her dogs on them. Nan Roberts (who just happened to be staying with us at the time) asked kindly how many times he had done it. "Oh lots," he replied with some bravado.

"Really? I only remember catching two little boys once, and yes, I did set the dogs on them, but they are so old, they don't have enough teeth to bite properly!" Alan had gone beet red on hearing her speak and finally recognising her. He started to slide down his dining chair until his head barely appeared above the table. Someone hurriedly changed the subject. What happenstance, to have the ex-wife of Wilfred Roberts (Lib. M.P.) at table with my young school friend, both some 240 miles from home!

On the weekends, we would get together in Hampstead.

He had metal-wheeled roller skates on which he would barrel down Willow Road with his bottle-green nylon cape flying behind him, leaving behind a metallic rattling rumble of noise. He also had a splendid train set on a table with electric trains that ran through a countryside of magical tiny scenery. He told me I should get one but I had to point out that we had no electricity. He would turn out the lights in his room and run the trains around their tracks with their lights on. Oh, the miracle of electricity! I wonder if he had a television? I doubt it, this was still early years for TV and I don't remember my friends talking about it until I was in high school. Alan was obviously spoiled with gifts and starved for affection and attention. When I saw him in New York in the early '70s I thought it was the last time – he was on the road with the Grateful Dead. His wife had left him for one of the writers (who later become his boss and friend) – he followed her… and later, I was told, he had O.D.'d, not impossible given the addictions of some of the band. Except that he had most definitely not died and never took that dangerous path! I discovered him again quite recently and having spoken first on the telephone, have since spent some very pleasant times together.

One Saturday when we were still in school together, he invited me to join him on Hampstead Heath for a 'war game'. We were fighting a large gang of older boys with several air rifles or BB guns… I do not remember whether there was anyone else on our side. Alan had an air rifle. We wriggled and crawled up to the crests of ridges and shot at the other side. They shot back. It was thrilling! Once or twice we were hit on our winter jackets and no harm was done, but now I wonder how losing an eye would have affected one of us. Sooner or later, I expect that someone did get hurt and the police would have been called in to keep an eye on the park. What really bothered me about the incident was that Father had trained me so strictly about guns.

Thinking back, I wonder what influence the boys' fathers

had on them, that they should play this war game. Since Father was too old for combat, he had that desk job in the Admiralty. Other, younger fathers – begetting while celebrating a brief leave or being wounded – would have seen combat, and many died even after procreating. Of those who came home, some would, no doubt, have suffered post traumatic stress syndrome (had it been labelled then), yet for many, serving their country was the high point of their lives. For them, the war was inconceivably intense, pushing them to their utmost physical and mental limits in ways that later desk jobs or manual labour would never ever do. I was born when Montgomery was making slow advances up the East coast of Italy: November 20, 1943. Germany's capitulation and the ceasefire came about eighteen months later. Despite such conflicting feelings about the episode, in the heat of the moment I thoroughly enjoyed the thrill of the game. It was only afterwards that it left a bad taste in my mouth. Father felt guilty that he had been too young to do active service in the First World War, too old for the Second, and would have gladly served, so he was hardly a pacifist, but he was profoundly anti-violence. When Norman Mailer raised his fists against Father at some literary event, Father just embraced him in a bear-hug until he calmed down and stopped kicking. At 1.90m and some 110 kg, he was a giant compared to Mailer.

Years earlier, I had caught double pneumonia. I must have been three or four at the time and my head was covered with pale-blond curls. There were no American servicemen in Wales, but when we visited Mother's family in Gloucestershire, in the West of England, there were still quite a few, left over from the war – Fairford remained an American base for many years.

Father once asked a local farm worker what he thought of these American GIs? The response was: "Oh, they's grand chaps, grand indeed… but I'm not so sure about them white fellows they bring along with 'em."

When these GIs drove past in their army trucks, they would shout good-naturedly at me: "Curly curly blondie". I hated what I took as the taunts and thought they were a reflection on my virility, at three or four years old? Yes, I thought they took me for a girl. I started plastering down my hair with water as Nino did with his oil, combing it back flat so that it did not curl. Wet hair in a stone, unheated house and cold winter weather outside, contributed to fell me with double pneumonia and I spent what seemed like an eternity in bed.

At the time, I was too young to read, but distracted myself with the *Ashley Book of Knots*. It had just come out and Father had an advance review copy. With some rope and a marlin spike, I learned to knot and splice rope before I could read – alas, synthetic ropes have done away with such skills, but at least they don't rot. Someone gave me my first factory-made toy: a cap pistol with rolls of pink paper caps which made it go 'bang' when fired. I once pointed it at Father when he came to visit me in bed – and 'shot' him. He was livid. He told me never ever to point a gun at anyone.

He brought up a 12-bore shotgun and showed me how to dismantle and clean it, without ever pointing it at anyone. He told me stories of the neighbourhood farm boys and how they were always shooting themselves in the foot because they did not keep the safety catch on, how they shot each other through sloppy practices. Just like a recent vice-president of America – the stupid farm-hand! He drilled into me that a gun was useful to get food (in our case, rabbits and wild duck) but lethally dangerous... and yet here I was on Hampstead Heath inviting older boys to shoot at me! Alan never lent me his gun, so I did not have to cross that line: shooting at someone else. I just invited others to take pot shots at me...

By the time of our trip to Bardsey, he was starting public school and I was still only in my prep school. After that I remember going to visit him when he was at Westminster

School in London. We were noticeably no longer friends and he seemed very grown-up to me, but his great sadness had seriously set in by then... he seemed depressed. His father had told him that it is hard for children to maintain their friendship, when one has passed puberty and moved on to a more grown-up situation and the other is still at a younger school. After Cambridge, he went to work at the Tavistock Institute where he was a visiting scholar. He spoke to me of Lang's theory of the acceptance of schizophrenia... but that was before I had read Lang. That was all to come.

For all Mother's scant control of her household, throughout our school lives, she somehow managed to send at least seven letters a week – or often postcards when she was abroad. One was for each of her five children, then one to her own mother and finally, one to her mother-in-law (Father couldn't bear the slightest contact with his own mother). They were distracted, scatty ramblings and barely legible at that. Remarkably straight lines of monotonous scribble, with clear, round loops for the letters L, G, B and D. They never ever answered any questions that I had asked in my own letters... they were simply regular affirmations that we existed. To this day, I like to receive bills, simply because they show that other people, out there, believe that I exist. No one writes letters any more. Living lonely and broke in Paris, I would take out my own passport to confirm my existence in the eyes of the world. In New York, I would re-read the letters (a dozen or so) that I myself had written to my Sponsors for Immigration purposes, so that they could simply have their secretaries copy the texts onto their own letterheads, sign and return them to me. Besides such Artists as Victor Vasarely, Julio Le Parc, François Morellet, Jack Youngerman, Schaeffer, Jacov Agam, there were letters 'from' Directors of the Tate Gallery, Joseph Hirshhorn, the Corcoran Gallery in Washington, Howard Wise in New York, the Gallery owner Denise Renée in Paris – they had all helped me by signing the letters I had written for them! Now they helped me by letting me confirm my own existence by reading their signatures on my letters. It does seem that I was skilled at fooling myself.

XVI

THE SAILING BUG

Father's first novel *A High Wind in Jamaica* (1928) spanned the interests of old and young alike. It took a great deal of research into the inner workings of children as they really are and not as the Victorian era, into which he was born (by just a year), sentimentally liked to imagine them. Since he was still a young bachelor at the time, he had borrowed a few children from friends, having them to stay for days or weeks and observing them. He told them stories, mining their own imaginations for further stories. I believe he spent a good deal of time with my two eldest siblings, but then the War came. Three more children arrived, then life, society, finances, home were all disrupted and everyone felt deracinated, even if they never left the British Isles and did not lose everything. Things were very different. Father never showed us younger children the same attention or interest that he had shown the pre-war generation of his offspring.

He was always so distant, untouchable, not to be disturbed – until there were other children visiting. Then he would do 'acrobatics' with us on the grass, spinning us around and catapulting us in somersaults over his shoulder, head first down his back, to be swung to and fro between his legs. I think I was jealous of these visitors who could elicit such attention from him, I imagined that he gave them more attention than he gave me in these games – though I am quite sure he was scrupulously fair. He even had some acrobatic skills with children in bed. Again they would be initiated when there were visiting kids, we would go to see him, all of us in pyjamas and he would bounce us on his foot while he lay flat on his bed and twirl us around with our back on his raised foot, always with a visitor, never for me alone. My siblings considered I was spoiled, as far as I am concerned, I was raised with his 'benign neglect'. Then too, there would be his bedtime stories in which he would ask us each to imagine a person, an animal or an object and he would weave a tale around the words we gave him. Later in life, he said that by morning he would have quite forgotten the story, but would go back to the children for their version of it. If it seemed worthwhile to him, he would write it down and many of them were later published in his collections of children's short stories.

As the youngest, many of my earlier years at home were spent alone. There were no stories for a single child. I would be put to bed and told not to wander about. Sometimes, after I had been told that the black labrador 'Lanta' was mine, I would ask for her to sleep in my room. Feeling lonely and sleepless, I would attach a note to her collar, asking for someone to come and say 'Goodnight'. I knew she would gravitate to the only fire burning in the house, in the dining-living room. The results were poor, since: a) I could not yet write, b) Lanta would inadvertently drop my note, c) the living room door was closed and she took the second-best solution: the warm kitchen range where cooking was already over and being consumed next door. So, I almost never got the attention I demanded and thought I deserved.

Father's next book was commissioned and was surely for adults only. *In Hazard* (1938) was also a best seller, to his surprise, even outselling his first, more notorious book. Then, during the War, the life he led in London, working for the Admiralty in a bombproof bunker off Pall Mall, was mostly male and certainly childless. At night, bedtime stories were replaced by rooftop vigils for fires, watching as the German bombers flew in to destroy their targets in London. In between the 'Jerries' came flights of wild duck, sweeping in on the lake in Regent's Park, but of course he could not start hunting them, he would have to wait for that until he moved back to Wales. Even after the War, first there was the pioneering move to North Wales, then back to London on more Admiralty work, then finally writing screen plays until Ealing Studios was sold up in the face of competition from T.V. Of course, with the will to do so, Ealing could have continued; television desperately needed studios, but the business was privately owned and the will was not there.

Small wonder, then, that Father was a changed man after the War, a man I never felt I knew, despite the fact that he was at home writing, gardening, fishing and even taking us sailing.

Yes, he took us sailing. Of course the tide had to be right – on the rise and high enough to float us over the nearest sandbanks. Then there had to be enough wind. After that, rain and even darkness were no deterrent. If you don't do what you want to do because it's raining in Wales, you will never do anything at all. For me, this started a lifelong love of sailing.

One night, we were out sailing with a three-quarter moon lighting our way and brilliant phosphorescence swirling behind us in our wake. When we hit a sandbank, he stripped off his trousers, leaving them rolled-up on the boat and jumped over the side. The phosphorescence swirled about again, lighting up his hairy legs like fairy's dust. We could see the outlines of the mountains and hills around and one bright oil lamp in the window of Mother's studio to guide us home. The tide was at its peak by now and we were off again, sailing well. The wind had freshened a little. Father was back in the boat, his pipe in his teeth, his beard jutting out and his great paw of a hand on the tiller. Suddenly we stopped again, but it was a different 'stop' to hitting a sandbank. He rushed forward, scattering children as he went, and leant over the side to see what the problem was. The next moment, he launched into one of his famous tirades in which he could continue cursing for several minutes on end without once repeating a phrase. He could swear with the rhythmic, inspired cadence of a Welsh preacher using the 'Hwyl', his anger and frustration matching the fire and brimstone lyric fury of a Minister's sermon. He had just sailed right into his own fishing nets! They were torn and a stake had been broken. It was indeed enough to make anyone furious at oneself.

He took us sailing in the daytime as well, when squalls of rain swept across the water, flattening the waves and stinging the face. He told me never to wear a cap, it would stop me feeling the wind. He showed me how to sail with my eyes closed, sensing the wind with my face and my skull. He showed me with amazing simplicity how the wind and sail work, how the sail luffs, or fills, or jibes – the balance of the boat and its sail to the wind, the delicate and perfect relationship created by the helmsman between his machine and the wind. He pointed out how you can watch the squall coming and anticipate its strength. All quietly, subliminally – unless we hit his nets – which we never ever did again! I became at least as passionate about sailing as he.

We had two sixteen-foot, open, clinker-built sailing boats. The old favourite was the (John) *Perrot* (after the Pembrokeshire, South Wales courtier – who could have been an illegitimate son of Henry VIII and who had six hundred Irish rebels executed in the sixteenth century – to encourage the others?). The other, a slightly faster, but very similar boat was called the *Amy*. Tradition holds that no boat could ever be renamed, so perhaps Amy was someone's teenage truelove. They had centreboards of cast iron, which could be lowered and held in place with a rusty nail through a series of holes that allowed adjustment to the depth of the plate. They felt as if they weighed a ton, at the age of seven I could barely drag one into position and hoist the top end so it would drop down the slot, so I did not, at first, use the centre-board when sailing alone... I just had to sail sideways. The iron centreboards were supposed to have handles welded onto them, but they had long since rusted away. Once, when sailing with my 'sailing' sister (the eldest), the rusty nail gave way and the centreboard fell through, but not all the way out. The remains of the handle stuck in the casing, thank goodness.

Meanwhile, the centreboard had also dropped into the sandbank beneath us – pinning us to the ground. I must have been quite young, I remember my sister explaining that I had to lift and hold the centreboard while she pushed it up from below. By the time her instructions were over, she was naked and over the side into the cold seawater. Under the boat, in perhaps five feet of water, she grabbed the centreboard and heaved it up again so that I could grab it. No longer pinned to the sandbank, we were off and under way before she was back on board. There was nothing I could do about trimming the gaff sail or our course, I was hanging on to a fifty pound plate of rusty iron with both hands! She leapt aboard, naked as a mermaid, grabbed the tiller as she dressed and we were on our way. We found another nail to hold up the centre-board and carried on as if nothing had happened. The sailing lesson was evident: act immediately, logically, whatever the discomfort – *just do it now!*

There was also a small, but heavy, ten-foot rowing dinghy used for fishing, rowing lessons and as an occasional rescue craft – if only for sheep stranded by a rising tide. All these boats had oars and oarlocks – rowlocks, as we called them. Sheep are extremely stupid and we were forever having to rescue them from the rising tide – just as mountain farmers are always having to rescue them from tiny ledges on precipices.

Often, after these mountain rescues, the sheep are slaughtered, because they only remember how sweet the grass on that impossible cliff-ledge was and go right back for it and get stuck again. I am sure they never learned about tides either and would get caught again, but I never heard of the local farmers slaughtering them after these sea rescues.

The highest, or 'spring' tides come two or three days after the full moon (thus monthly). Then the rise and fall was at its greatest. There were secondary spring tides after the new moon, but they would be at least four feet lower. The spring tides waned to 'neap' tides where the rise and fall was at its minimum. The vernal and autumnal equinoxes added an extra few feet to the highest tides, as did a heavy south-west gale. Tidal waves or tsunamis were probably caused by offshore seismic activity – there had been one in 1933. As for the timing of the twice-daily tides, spring tides rose about 35 minutes later each time and neap tides about 50 minutes later. Thus there is a continual progression in time as well as in height... forever changing like the seasons and the sun's rising and setting. All chronicled to within a minute in the precious Tide Tables.

XVII

NOW HOOKED ON SAILING

When my Parents had lived in South Wales in the thirties, there had also been the *Dauntless* – an eighteen-foot clinker-built boat that was relatively fast for the time. The mast was stepped too far forward, making her fast to windward, but very liable to 'sail under' (basically, to dive) and also to capsize when jibing while running before the wind.

There was a story of how my Parents took Mother's mother and her second husband out for a sail. He had been commissioned as a commander in the Royal Navy. He insisted on taking the helm from Father, pulling rank on him. Father warned him not to let her jibe when running before the wind, but of course he was ignored as a 'junior officer'. Jibe they did and immediately capsized some three miles offshore. Picture the 1930s gentry in boating gear of blazers and ties, long white dresses and sunhats, very wet, hatless, sitting on the hull of the upturned boat – Father's pipe still in his teeth, waving politely to a passing fishing boat which came to their aid. The *Dauntless* was excommunicated forever by Mother and I never saw more than her dried-up hull in South Wales and a few photographs.

Father, incidentally, would not have been stylishly dressed. Even back in those days, he wore old flannel trousers rolled up to the knee and a heavy cable-knit sweater full of holes. Indeed, in the twenties and thirties, he went to great lengths to ask friends in America to send him pale blue shirts with collars attached. When I childishly pointed out to him that he had said: "Before the War, only cads wore anything but a white shirt," he just looked at me with that twinkle in his eye that meant: "Make of it what you will."

The queen of the fleet was the *Tern* – a 25-foot fully-decked fishing-boat that had been converted into a 'yacht'. She had brass-framed portholes and standing room below decks for anyone less than 5'0" short. Two berths were also the seats in the saloon, the fo'c'sle was just a sail and chain locker. She was very slow and very seaworthy and, captained by Father in the thirties, had been the only contestant in the Bristol Channel Pilots' Race to finish – the other contestants fled for port or were dismasted in a gale. The pilot assigned to the *Tern* was an elderly alcoholic with a mortal fear of heavy weather, who stayed below with the ship's rum and was of no use whatsoever in the treacherous shoals of the Bristol Channel. The victor's great silver trophy is still in the family, the date: 1936.

Just before the War, Father brought the *Tern* up from Laugharne in South Wales to Porthmadog in the North (a couple of hundred miles by sea, not counting tacking). He had his friend and sailing partner Jack Rowlands along as crew. Father, like many Britons, assumed that Hitler's advance was unstoppable and that once France was defeated, he would not halt at the English Channel, but invade the British Isles as well. Father decided that if that came about, he could hole up with his family in the mountains of North Wales, and having the *Tern* at hand made complete sense. At a pinch, he could have sailed the family over to Ireland (which remained neutral during what the Irish called 'The Emergency'). Indeed, he had stocked the old house, Parc, with large quantities of canned and dried food for just such an eventuality. It came in useful after the War, while rationing still continued.

Tern had a full keel and drew 3½ feet, so at low water, she either lay very sadly on her side on the sand or was fitted with 'crutches' on either side. It was rare that the tides were high enough to float her. My eldest sister went onboard her in Porthmadog and actually spent the night aboard. Later writing of her lifelong passion for sailing that started at that moment when she peeped out of a porthole and saw the cottages of the town, almost from sea level and felt the gentle rocking as she laid at anchor. My brother recalls arduous days scraping off old paint, caulking between the seams and repainting her. He said she was in a sorry state after being out of water for the duration of the War. I too remember playing on board, both when she was lying over on her side and when she was floating on a very high tide. Finally she went back to Porthmadog and I never saw her again. I never again knew such an intense old smell of tar, nor felt the prickly scratch of either henequen (sisal) or hemp rope as I remember from the *Tern*. The boats I sailed on ever afterwards had man-made fibre ropes and tar was replaced with epoxy for hulls.

In the mid-1920s, Father had sailed to Ireland on a Porthmadog slate schooner. He told me how, when going about or tacking, he would put the helm hard down, secure it with a twist of rope, go forward to change side on the jib sheets, stop by the galley on the way back to the helm just to stir the soup on the stove and make sure it wasn't sticking, return in a leisurely manner to the helm, release the rope holding the helm, right her and set the new course according to the set of the sails. Working on a big heavy wooden hulled schooner was not a hurried affair and they were engineered not by theory but by generations of sea-faring practice.

Years later I crewed on a Bristol Channel Pilot Cutter of 40 tons, built in the late nineteenth century, from Dover to Amsterdam and back. At fourteen, I could handle her alone on the night shifts, tacking and all. I felt tremendously empowered to be driving this beautiful old machine across the ocean. She was designed exactly for that: a teenage boy could manage her by himself in most situations, foresails and all.

Around that time (in the mid-20s) after Father had sailed to Ireland on that slate boat, he went down to the dock in Porthmadog to see off another slate schooner. He had almost signed on with her, but then thought there would be many more occasions on other ships to do so. However, she was the last slate ship to leave the dock. She had a figurehead of a young girl in a navy blue tunic school uniform. The 'model' for the schoolgirl was there on the dock to see her off too – by then she was a heavy, matronly grandmother! The good ship was gone three years and finally ended her days three miles inshore after a hurricane in the tropics, having crisscrossed the ocean trading hither and yon. He had lost his opportunity to crew on the last ship out of Porthmadog. You can talk of 20-20 hindsight, but it would be more productive to speak of seizing the day. Besides, even if he didn't stay on board until the hurricane finally destroyed her, he could easily have been lost overboard in the interim – it happened all the time. In which case, neither I nor my siblings nor his novels would have seen the light of day.

The watershed occasion, as far as sailing was concerned, was the first time I went sailing by myself. There was a little wind and the tide was very high. I asked Mother if I might go. She asked Father. I think I overheard him say: "Why not? He ought to know what he's doing by now. It's time he started learning on his own." Of course the 'why not' could also have been 'why now?' These boats were extremely heavy and a child of seven or eight could never push one off a sandbank. But it was never said. Even raising the gaff sail was very hard work for me, and the centreboard very nearly beyond my powers (even with a new nail to hold it in place). I became adept at jumping overboard the instant I touched bottom and hauling her about, to sail off the bank. That way, I avoided the need for the brute force that I did not have. I don't know what age I was, but it was an extraordinary lesson in managing something far heavier and more powerful than myself. It could have been a racehorse or a high-powered car, but it was an old sailing boat. I was addicted. It seemed such a wonderful machine to me, powered as it was by the wind.

Father was mostly very calm and laconic. He did not praise, but if he approved of something one did, he would look a little to the side with a twinkle in his eyes, as if a little embarrassed to acknowledge something well done. Mother, on the other hand, remains a highly colourful character in my mind, but I don't believe I was close to her either. That I remained their only unmarried child through the 60s and came home regularly was through a sense of duty that had become ingrained in me. Not, I believe, because of filial love. I have been told by my siblings that she doted on me and spoiled me. She may well have doted on me, but she also ignored me. She would praise me and then rub in how much more brilliant they were. Eccentric and scatter-brained, she could be over-protective and yet forget I existed completely.

I sought desperately to please my Parents and adventuresome travel was certainly one way of impressing them. Not that they ever remarked much upon my wanderings. It would be much later that I revolted and then, because I was older, the revolt was all the stronger. I recall referring to my Parents as 'the Fossils', though such disdain was skin-deep. Like them or not, my respect for them was unquestionable...

I could scarcely have had more liberty, yet I always knew that I could come home to a bed (not always a warm or particularly dry one) and a square meal. We children were neglected to do as we liked – and what a choice we had – yet the 'benign' element was always there. I was twenty six when, for the first time ever, I cabled Father to borrow £10, in Sweden, because I had nothing left to pay for petrol in order to return the car I had borrowed from a friend in France. Naturally I repaid him, but he was astonished that I even had to ask him, after the tens of thousands of miles I had already covered without going broke. Being responsible for a car is an expensive proposition. A person may go without food or lodging, but a car will just go no further when the tank is empty. His surprise was the greatest compliment he had ever indulged in me.

It may seem strange that my family remains faceless and nameless. We all went away to boarding school as early as possible (in my case, seven). My brother is exactly eleven years my senior, so he was an almost grown-up, angry young man in my eyes during that fifties era of the 'Angry Young Men' like John Osborne. My next older sibling, a sister, is three and a half years older than I. There are two more older sisters in between. We sometimes crossed each other's paths during holidays, but for most of those first they, then I, were away from home. We were working or just staying with one or other of our extended family. Yes, I went on a riding trip with the sister closest to me in age, but she had much more in common with our next older sister. My eldest sister was closer to our brother (the eldest of all) and anyway, all five of us were encouraged to be independent. Nowadays, they have indeed become my friends, very special, close friends. But it took retirement and old age to get to know them.

Father left us in our own 'benign neglect', while Mother seemed quite bemused by her role. Clearly, she far preferred to cook a dinner for interesting adults than prepare fuel for children. She did take some interest in us once we could talk and discuss things – babies were of little interest to her. Nor could she remember our names; she often called me Crumbface for my messy eating habits as a toddler. Not that I think such amnesia is rare amongst harassed mothers, but she was especially, extraordinarily forgetful...

Thus, my memories are of solitude, endless solitude, solitude alone, solitude in a crowd, even solitude with one other person. I would never learn to feel that I understood what made other people tick. After some forty years of marriage (on and off), I know in an uncanny way what my spouse is thinking at any one moment... but I have not a clue why she is thinking that way, nor why indeed I have come to the same thought myself.

Oh yes, I have some happy memories of when most or all of my siblings and our Parents did something together. I do remember being crammed into the back of that tiny Willys Army Jeep with my four siblings. We were all dressed as Cowboys and Red Indians. The Jeep had been painted with scenes of the Wild West (which remained for many years to come...) and we were on the way to a nearby carnival. Once there, we children climbed on the roof and bonnet or hood of the Jeep, uttering fearsome war cries in our high voices, while our Parents drove us sedately in the parade.

There was the time when my brother had just returned from his first trip to Bavaria (to improve his German) and brought me a little pair of Lederhosen in which I nevertheless floated. Luckily, Lederhosen have braces or suspenders, so they didn't fall to the ground. Two of my lovely sisters decided that the true test of Lederhosen would be.... To be swung by my arms and legs higher and higher and then cast onto the top of a gorse bush – gorse being famous for being a mass of thorns, except just where they bloom, when beautiful little deep yellow blossoms are added to the spikes. Oh yes, the Lederhosen were impeccable in their protection of those parts they protected. Beyond that frontier, my martyrdom was far more general than a mere crown of thorns.

Another time a whole crowd of us (perhaps not all my siblings, but house guests as well) celebrated two of my sisters' birthdays, besides our Father's, on Puffin Island, also named Saint Tudwel's Island West. A fisherman took us out from Abersoch to the tiny rock crowned with a lighthouse that we could enter. We ate our picnic on the circular balcony that ringed the tower just below the light. Built in 1877, there were lighthouse keepers' cottages besides the lighthouse itself. At that time, the cottages were abandoned, for the light had been converted to electricity and was controlled from the land.

A nearby island, Saint Tudwal's Island East, has a priory on it dating from the sixth century (much the same date as the monastery on Bardsey Island (516 AD) and was used for bombing practice during World War II.

Looking down from the lighthouse parapet, it seemed that there was almost no island around us, we looked almost straight down to the rocks and waves. The rocks were covered in seals that were fascinated by our intrusion, looking inquisitively at us and loudly discussing us with each other. There were rabbit warrens in the shallow earth but most of the rabbits had been evicted by nesting puffins. We were sternly warned not to put our hands down the burrows to look for puffins' eggs – the bite of the puffin's parrot-like beak could sever your finger.

At the end of the picnic, the birthday cake appeared and it was then that we realised we had forgotten to bring candles. Resourceful as ever, Mother produced some bananas – what did the quantity matter at a time like this? She peeled them and stuck them unceremoniously into the cake, then a match stick in the top of each from Father's pipe tobacco pouch, the whole shielded from the wind by rain ponchos… and voila! We had candles after all. Blowing them out in one puff was greatly facilitated by the removal of the ponchos.

For another family picnic, we went to a cottage that my brother had rented for a summer holiday, so he could study in peace, with a few friends from his public school (Eton). He paid the rent out of his salary of two pounds a week as editor of the school newspaper. He was walking in the footsteps of our Father, who himself had moved out of his mother's house in southeast England and rented a one-room cottage in Wales, quite near where we now lived. My brother's cottage was only accessible by the then defunct Ffestiniog Railway. We drove to the nearest station, Tan-y-Bwlch (then occupied as a holiday cottage), with its cast-iron bridge nearby dated 1854. There we took the small railway wagon that came with the cottage. Some adults walked, the babies like myself were piled on the wagon with the picnic. The dogs followed panting in the heat of the day. One adult pushed the wagon to get it rolling uphill and then jumped on board and poled it along with ease, using a broomstick.

Below the station, the vegetation is still lush to this day, thick with forests of rhododendron under a mixture of huge, mature deciduous trees (oak, ash and beech), but from the station on up, the landscape turns suddenly to bare heath, with rocks, heather and occasional bracken. So my brother's rented house was in rough upland summer grazing for sheep.

The 60 cm gauge track for this railway was built with a constant 1:80 grade all the way from Porthmadog, the harbour on the coast, up to Blaenau Ffestiniog, where the slate quarries thrived. First used in 1844, ponies pulled the empty wagons up to the quarries (13½ miles) and then rode back down in a small horsebox (munching from their hay nets) with the loaded train, powered by gravity alone. In 1863, steam engines were introduced and the ponies retired. Two years later, passenger coaches were introduced to transport workers, but soon farmers and their wives joined them as well for shopping expeditions to Porthmadog. In 1939, with the onset of War, the railway closed down and stayed closed throughout my childhood. Now it has been restored as a tourist attraction, and a spectacular ride it is.

Porthmadog remained the main shopping town of my youth, and I remember the two old sisters who still drove into town once a week in the car they had bought brand new in 1929. They were a little hard of hearing, but shared a beautiful old 'hearing' horn. It was black and bound with silver bands... perhaps it was the horn of a buffalo or a cow – but they took it in turns to hold the sharp end to their better ear, so a friend could shout the latest scandal down the broad end. Everyone within three blocks could hear what was said, and then heard it again when the other sister put the horn to her ear.

Then, there was also David Lloyd George's younger

brother William, who had taken over his illustrious brother's law practice in 1887 and still insisted (at age ninety-nine) on going to the office every day – throwing the whole place into chaos by asking for files that had been settled half a century before (or so it was said).

We reached the cottage and explored its somewhat barren interior. It had been sparsely furnished, though I think my brother must have borrowed a few more pieces of furniture. Once, while rummaging in some drawers and closets, he came upon some private, handwritten letters, addressed to Kim Philby, one of the 'Cambridge Five': Philby, Donald MacLean, Guy Burgess, Anthony Blunt and perhaps John Cairncross. They were Russian spies who had been Marxists at Cambridge in the 1930s, and some of them defected to Russia (when their covers had been blown) between 1951 and '63. One of them was related to us by marriage, though he did not defect and avoided prosecution, probably through 'good gay connections' – disgrace was harder to evade. Mother complained that he had been an intellectual snob as a young man and refused to dance with young flappers like herself. She had not noticed at the time that he was homosexual, which could well have explained how choosey he was with his dancing partners.

Then, Father had been close friends with Sir Dick White (who probably came to some of those parties at Carlton Mews), first Head of MI5 and then MI6, who probably ordered the diver Captain Crabb to investigate the propeller of the Soviet cruiser that brought Khrushchev to Britain (he disappeared, either defected, shot by the Soviet sailors on board or killed by his diving partner because he knew too politics and East-West espionage had reached even this far into this remote cottage on a hot summer's day in North Wales… James Bond never deigned to visit the area, but his real-life colleagues most certainly did!

The honey bees buzzed lazily in the heather flowers amongst the rocks and the scent of dry herbs hung in the heat as we dozed lazily after lunch and before the trek back down the railway line to the station where the jeep was parked. Downhill, the wagon coasted by itself; it no longer had brakes so stopping its gentle progress took some adult strength.

XVIII

PONY TREKKING

On the horse front, 1954 was to be my last equine experience for many years. Mother sent my youngest sister and myself on a pony trek. My sister must have been twelve or thirteen and I, about ten. We made lists of things to pack and loaded everything into makeshift saddlebags and two small knapsacks for our own backs. We had read of Western horsemen carrying 'bed rolls', but sleeping bags and modern tents do not drape so conveniently over the pommel. Our saddles were conventional English ones, devoid of hooks for tying things on, so we would be continuously having to pull things up straight again. I was to ride our stolid old Welsh grey mountain pony, Nancy. My sister had borrowed a black, skittish three-year-old gelding that was scarcely broken in yet. Our Mother told us exactly where we were to spend the first, second and third nights and promised she would meet us by car on the second day, to see if we were all right. That way we would not need to carry a change of clothes. Naturally, by the time we could read and write, we knew how to map read and no doubt an adult had helped choose our route, so there would be a minimum of roads – which are dangerous on horseback, besides being boring and not at all adventuresome.

We were told to stop at the blacksmith's shop to have Nancy's shoes tightened and the colt shoed for the first time. We were wary of blacksmiths having heard of the altercation

Father had had with another, recalcitrant one.

Under duress, he had agreed to come to the house to shoe an old racehorse with a broken wind (from being galloped full out by a stable hand when she was only two years old) besides a pony as well. When he said he did not have a car, Father offered to come and pick him up and he accepted. Father arrived at the designated hour, only to find the smith busy with other work. The smith refused to come with him, saying he had a lucrative job to do in his own shop and he'd prefer to stay there. Father tried to argue about one's word and something known as 'commitment', but the smith just became angry, threatening to fight Father over the matter. He took one look at the smith's huge forearms and work-hardened hands and declined, with the words: "Sir, the hands that wield the pen are no match for those that wield the hammer on the anvil." Surprisingly, the blacksmith capitulated, sulkily climbing into the old American Army Jeep with his tools – but he never uttered a word and Mother had to find a more obliging smith in the future, so it was to this kinder man that we were to go.

We were lucky with the weather, but I was not entirely enthusiastic about this trip. First, it was the horses. Then, I had not chosen this adventure and my sister seemed to have absorbed all our Mother's huge enthusiasm for herself. Lastly, as if I were not already captive on an expedition, Nancy was as pig-headed and bossy as a dozen mothers and sisters.

Once, when Nancy bit another sister on the bridge of the nose, removing her frown for ever, the sister turned and tried to bite her back, hard on the hindquarters... she came away with her mouth so full of thick pony fur that it looked as if she'd swallowed her own grey beard. Not only that, but pony skin is mostly stretched too tight to get a decent bite in with human teeth, so the attempted counter-attack held neither satisfaction for her, nor retribution for Nancy. My pretty sister looked funny with a grey beard, she had asked for it and now she had it. The blood running down from the frown at the bridge of her nose, was less amusing, though there was no drama, no doctors, no stitches and it healed – though she still cannot frown!

I twice saw Nancy discomfited: once on a summer's day, when all the doors were wide open for the breeze, she came into the kitchen and devoured a whole dish of sandwiches prepared for some illustrious guest at teatime. Caught red-hoofed, she was cursed roundly, and guiltily tried to make her hurried exit through the front hall. Unfortunately, iron shoes on smooth tile are like skates on ice. She slithered to and fro and knocked the Italian marble mosaic table in the hall to the ground, smashing it to a million pieces. It took the introduction of Epoxy glue and a couple of kind artist friends a couple of winter months to restore.

The other time was when I saw Nancy desperately cleaning her teeth on the top of the half-door in the stable. It was designed for larger horses and Nancy, at 12.2 hands, could hardly reach it with her teeth, let alone hang her whole head and neck out as larger horse would. She looked pathetic and I confess that I was glad to see her plight – nasty, sadistic little boy that I was. My sisters had decided to make toffee but overcooked it until it was more like caramel. They tried it on our Father who promptly lost two teeth in it, so they tried it on Nancy... who simply loved it, until she got her own teeth stuck together and was forced to try and clean them off on the stable door.

So I was not going to be really riding Nancy, so much as she was going to be taking me for a three-day ride, with incessant pit-stops to savour tufts of grass along the way – inevitably throwing the bag on the pommel of the saddle over her neck so that it hung about her ears. At least Nancy was so unflappable that she didn't seem to mind having a bag on her head as she ate, as long as I didn't annoy her by pulling on the reins and trying to interrupt her snack.

We took the way up the estuary, much as the Koestlers

had, in order to get back to their car after dinner, though we kept further out than the sea grass, where streams had eroded deep gullies. On a normal day, we would have enjoyed jumping these little ravines, but inefficiently loaded as we were, we knew that a jump would mean losing our camping gear in brackish water. We rode carefully around to where the original road to our house had been along the shore. Half a mile or so of it had been washed away by a great tidal wave in the 1930s and never repaired since... The tidal wave had flooded farmland that had not been sea for the last few hundred years. When people alighted from the evening train during the tidal wave, at the local 'halt' or un-staffed platform with room for just one carriage, it was already pitch dark and the little platform was surrounded by water. Since this is Wales, the natural reaction was that this was the end of the world. Everyone started singing hymns in four part harmony... until rowboats appeared out of the night to take people home to their houses. A friend in the village of Ynys was born that very night and so was always known as 'Mary Mor Don' or 'Mary Sea Wave' – she was born upstairs at home and her parents found stranded flat fish on the floor of the kitchen when they came down in the morning! I would surely have forgotten her story, had I not happened to attend her funeral quite recently. Appropriately enough, the eulogy included the story of her birth. In the Baptism Registry she is even recorded as 'Mary Mordon Roberts'.

From there, we had half a mile of asphalt, across the flats that had once been sea, past the train 'halt' (scene of the supposed apocalypse) and then up a track into the hills. My sister's pony found everything new and frightening. He shied at a bee, a stream in the valley below, the glinting of the sun through the oak leaves – anyone would think he'd never been for a walk in his life. He did all the worrying for plodding, phlegmatic Nancy, who couldn't care a hoot.

Soon we were above the tree line and cutting north along the Roman Road, which was surely much older than the

Romans. By late morning (we had started at dawn), we were down from the high land and crossed the river Afon (river in Welsh) Dwyryd (which fed our branch of the estuary, the Traeth Bâch, or Small Beach) using the stone bridge at Maentwrog for the crossing and so reached the blacksmith's shop. This was an important scheduled stop because the young pony had never been shod before and would need shoes for riding so far and hard, especially on roads.

The blacksmith might just as well have been Joe from Dickens's *Great Expectations*. Like ourselves, he did not have electricity and used a hand bellows as he worked. He was rail-thin with great knots of sinew and muscle rippling up and down his bare arms. He had a full head of wavy grey hair and a way of whistling in two parts, the tenor part coming from his side teeth and the alto from his lips. Like Joe, he too 'did not have his letters'. Father had once done a meticulous drawing of a pair of strap hinges he needed for the well cover, but when he showed them to the blacksmith, he was impatient and just said: "I never had my letters. Tell me what you want and I'll remember the size until my dying day." "Oh no," cried Father, "you mean it's going to take you that long to make them?" He was reassured that if he went for a pint, they'd be ready afterwards. I happen to know that the pint Father would drink would be a bottle of Worcester Sauce with a Guinness chaser. That was his well-known foible.

So the young pony led us on quite a dance. He kicked incessantly, until the blacksmith told me to hold up the hoof diagonally across from the one he was working on. Meanwhile, my sister held his head down to stop him rearing. That way, he could no longer kick – for, try as he might, he simply could not stand on one leg to kick! Like so many animals, horses cannot bear ridicule and the very thought of falling flat on his face, forced him to calm his protests. Nevertheless, it took a full three hours to shoe him – even with the blacksmith's calming whistle in harmony. Nancy, on the other hand, was ready to go in a few minutes and couldn't wait to be back out of the forge and in the land of green grass again.

We finally picked up the continuation of the Roman Road along the high ground above the tree line. In places there were large paving stones (which the ponies avoided as one avoids a patch of ice). They could have been laid by the Romans when they came to try and conquer the Welsh, but the road must also have seen two millennia of repairs. Alas, today it has been asphalted over, though it is still single track.

I sat, tired and mindless on Nancy, brought back to consciousness from time to time when she veered off the track to check out another tuft of grass. I would pull on her reins as hard as I could and she would do her best to ignore me. Suddenly I realized that the knapsack on my back was empty. It had split open at the bottom and gradually disgorged its contents, bit by bit over the last six miles.

My sister, ready to take command, said she would sew it up again... until we saw that the sewing kit had been in my pack! It had also contained what snacks we might have had, some apples and perhaps even a little precious chocolate. The visit to the blacksmith had taken so long, that it was getting late, and though the sun would only set at ten o'clock (being summer and this far north), we did not now have time to go back in search of a few small possessions. We rode on dejectedly to the farm where we were to camp for the night and graze the horses. It was down on the edge of the flat land at the bottom of the hills and we were exhausted when we finally reached it and introduced ourselves to the farmer.

He showed us the paddock with an old bathtub as a drinking trough, where we could leave the ponies for the night. We pitched our tent quickly (we had often practised when we went camping for a night on the hills near home) and walked off to the village of Gareg in search of food.

XIX

A SHEPHERD SWIMS

When our Mother had set us on our way, she had casually mentioned that she had no cash on her and that we would have to charge things we needed, such as grazing and food for ourselves. Since credit cards did not yet exist, we would have to ask vendors to give us credit, to send our Mother a bill and she would pay it. Such a request would have been perfectly normal in those days.

Few people carried much cash – nowadays, armed with a small plastic card, things can be easier – though they may encourage profligacy!

We went straight to the village shop, but of course it was closed (it must have been after 8 pm). The only other business that might have any food was 'Yr Ring', the pub. We were much too young to be allowed in and Mother disapproved of such places, but we went around to the kitchen door at the back. The English called it The Brondanw Arms, after the large house (or 'Plâs') where Clough and Amabel Williams-Ellis lived, but it was a hotbed of Welsh Nationalism, and they stubbornly called it 'Yr Ring' and only Welsh was spoken at the bar.

The back door was opened by the publican's wife and my sister explained our predicament. She told us to wait a moment while she talked to her husband, and soon came back and ushered us into her kitchen, sat us down with beer mugs full of milk and started cooking a feast for hungry children:

fried bangers (sausages), eggs, bubble-and-squeak (fried potato and cabbage) and fried bread. She was making us 'tea' and that was probably what anyone nearby with enough money would be eating. Not that they were fat, they walked everywhere and most were manual labourers. As we ate, she gently asked us a few questions and from time to time went out to the bar – from which came the sound of hymns being sung in Welsh, telling us that a good time was being had out there. Once one has reached that degree of inebriation, the morose stage, there's nothing like a good hymn sung in four-part harmony to drown the soul in melancholy. She would come back with beer mugs to wash at the kitchen sink, then she would wipe her hands on her apron and chat a little more.

After a while, the publican came in and sat at the kitchen table with us. My sister at once repeated what she had already told his wife: that he should send a bill to our mother and she would pay by cheque. He was a big man with a florid face. Though his size was intimidating, he was not unkind. He stopped her in mid-sentence and said: "Now then, nippers, I'm wanting to tell you a tale…"

We rested our knives and forks and looked at him.

"I was about your ages back then. Living on a hill sheep farm with me dad, me mam and nain [grandmother]. I was walking to school in Croesor and helping out on the farm before and after, like. Well, one summer, there's this tall young Englishman with a beard comes to live up here from time to time. Was it Garreg Fawr he was to living at? Well, doesn't matter. So this fellow gets to talking to us nippers and he says it's hot, how about we all go down to the beach to swim with him? Well some of us says yes and others says no, but I went along. He had this big Bentley car and he loads us in like sheep, all on top of each other. Five in the dickey, four in the seat beside him. I'd never been down to the beach. What would a sheep farmer be doing on the beach? Well he starts to teach us to swim.

"After that, when it was hot and we could get away, some

of us would go down there again with him and he'd teach us some more. He used to lie under water and we'd all sit on him to stop him coming up, but he was strong and sooner or later he would always come back up to breathe. After that summer, I never did run into him again, though they say he married and was living in Plas Parc for a while. Then the War came and I was called up. Then I was at Dunkirk. The boats could- n't come in too close for the Jerries' bombing and strafing at them, like. Hell's inferno, it was – *Diawchedig* [devilish]. I must 'a swum a mile out and was picked up by this little pleasure boat. He'd come over with the fishing boats and Navy boats and all. He took me out to a troop carrier that brought me home. Then he went right back inshore for more chaps. I often wonder to this day: did he make it home? Plucky fellow, that one." He paused with the innate Welsh instinct for drama and drew on the cigarette we had not seen him light.

"A sheep farmer, on the hills, me, what would I be having with the sea and with swimming if it wasn't for that Englishman? Nothing! Nothing, I tell you! Never would I have learned to swim without your father to teach me. I owe him my life. So finish up your tea, nippers, and don't be bothering me with no payments…" With that he was gone back to his customers, leaving us reeling with thought.

"*Well*," breathed his wife as the door closed, "and he never told me nothing about the War and all that. Probably wants to forget it all, I expect."

We thanked her profusely and she told us not to forget what her husband had told us. I, for one, never have. We walked back to the farm in the gathering dusk and by the time we had crept into our sleeping bags, replete and exhausted, it was dark and we had found a new respect for our Father. We learned much of our Father from the tales of others.

Next day, we rode back up to the Roman Road and continued on north, meeting our Mother at the next river crossing where we had to come down to the road for its bridge. She had forgotten our clean clothes (not that we noticed) but brought us some urgently-needed cash! She drove behind us as we crossed the bridge and followed the road up the side of a spectacular gorge with a raging torrent at the bottom (the River Glaslyn, that fed the other, reclaimed, branch of the estuary, the Traeth Mawr or Big Beach). Traffic was a nightmare, with noisy tourist buses belching smoke at us and practically shaving our legs off as they passed. Even the tourist cars were no better. Nancy was cool as a cucumber, but my sister's mount became so crazed, she had to jump off and lead him, her legs stiff from riding for hours.

After the gorge, we soon left the road and our Mother, and followed the disused track of a narrow gauge slate railway. The rails had been pulled up during the War for scrap metal, but many of the sleepers were still there and the ponies kept tripping on them. Nancy managed better and I just gave her her head and let her work it out. I was dreaming of being somewhere else – probably driving a car!

That night (we left the abandoned railway as soon as we could), we camped at another farm and offered to pay for our grazing. Two such young children, alone on horseback, were sufficiently unusual in those days for the farmer to refuse any payment. His wife even brought us some scones she had just baked. We ate the provisions we had bought before leaving the road... probably canned sausages and beans, if I remember.

The next day was another long ride. There was no more Roman Road and we juggled tracks and short pieces of small road. Here, the hills were lower, rounder, more tamed. The sunny weather held, but nothing much interested me and I sat watching Nancy's furry ears, nodding with her paces, just awake enough to grab the reins when she went for a tuft of grass. That evening, we arrived at the farm of some friends and they showed us a good camping spot. Our Mother arrived just as we were pitching the tent. She busied herself with setting up a plate-drying rack made of sticks in the ground. There was a water trough nearby which we shared with the ponies.

I was getting anxious now. All along I had known that the son of our friend the farmer had a home-made sports car that looked like a cigar on wheels. I couldn't wait to ride in it. Next day, we learned that he was away and his car with him. Mother spent time with the farmer's wife, my sister with her daughter Diana and I sulked. Finally, the farmer announced that he was taking a cattle truck down south to get some sheep and he could give the ponies a ride back. My sister and I rode with him. I was thankful and relieved not to be riding all the way back! Travel in one direction opens new horizons; return along your own footsteps and you see it all again. I have always tried to travel in some kind of loop.

XX

MY VERY OWN TRIP

I was getting wanderlust, but it had to be journeying according to my own desires. Before leaving on the pony trek, I had met three brothers, whose family had rented our cottage for a holiday. One was younger than I, the other two, older. They had invited me to stay with them in England, five or six hours' drive away, when I returned. At once I started making plans, assuming that I would just hitch-hike there. I was ten years old at the time.

Somehow, for once, my Parents united forces to find another way for me to go there. They did not come out and say I could not hitch. Mother just spent some time on the telephone and found a friend who was leaving for that part of the world, but from a town already two hours away. Telling me that I could not refuse the friend's 'kind offer', I was put on a train for the first leg. I spent the night at their house – he was Provost of a university and resigned soon afterwards, when his Board of Directors announced that 'students of colour' would not be accepted... this was deep in Wales and virtually no non-Caucasians would apply for many years to come, anyway. That was in the mid-fifties and eventually the issue came to the fore and, like it or not, universities were then obliged to accept any qualifying student.

Thus, the Provost (Goronwy Rees) was vindicated, but by then he was already a highly successful journalist and writer. Eventually too he was accused of being a Russian spy – an accusation that was never proven but upset him and his family no end.

Next day, Mrs Rees drove me further down and across Wales to the rich farming area of the Marches. I had always been told that the land was so called for the Roman sentries who marched up and down, keeping an eye on the Welsh and making sure they stayed in the highlands where the land was poor – nowadays, there are different theories, such as they were called Marches for the Marcher Lords who were given land along the frontier. Later Offa's Dyke was built in segments, which may have been joined by wooden palisades (which have long since disappeared – since they were made of wood). Up north, the Romans had built Hadrian's Wall to keep out the 'Barbarians' (Picts and Scots). The Welsh border, however, was much longer, so no wall was envisioned until Offa's Dyke. Instead they had patrols marching up and down the lowland side of the border – hence The Marches. Nevertheless, the Welsh, having been forced west out of their own rich farm land, frequently came down with raiding parties to help themselves to some fat cattle, sheep or goats. Their animals could not be fattened, because they had been reduced to such poor, upland grazing.

Mrs Rees drove an enormous American car that was, of course, left-hand drive. For the passenger, facing oncoming traffic on narrow Welsh roads that were almost completely blocked by this huge automobile, was terrifying. It was good training for the days when I would be hitch-hiking and accepted any ride I could get, however hair-raising it turned out to be.

Going back to the Marches: since I went away to school, in Wales I was considered to be English. The neighbouring children steered clear of me and when Mother invited them for tea, they were shy and embarrassed. Small wonder, I remember teasing one boy about his accent, making him blush at table. No one stopped me and I may well have found the idea in my English school. The Welsh boys mocked me behind my back for living in a 'Plâs' or mansion. While in English schools, first I was nicknamed 'Misty Mountain' – which I took as a compliment, though coming as it did from my teachers, it surely meant that I never paid attention in class.

"Taffy was a Welshman, Taffy was a thief,"

"Taffy came to my house and stole a leg of beef…"

Which was surely a mind-set that goes back to the Marches, during Roman times. Then the Saxons and after them the Norman Conquest of England, reinforced the same attitude and wealthy Normans took over the rich farms of the Marches. Gradually, the Welsh were considered second-class citizens because they were not as rich as the English, because the land they lived on was poor, because that was where successive invasions had pushed them. Instead of monetary wealth they became known for, and proud of, their literary, poetic and choral traditions. Their Bards were heroes. The Latin Bible was illegally translated from Latin into Welsh, 141 years before the King James English Version was translated. On the whole, I had no objection to being called a Welshman and hardly noticed the downside of the implied attribute: dishonesty, deviousness, and plain criminality. Not to mention that 'welshing' on an agreement is common usage to this day.

Still, the idea of being different, inferior, certainly formed me and I chose my few school friends from amongst those who lived overseas and rarely went home, those who had lost a parent and were neglected and other misfits like myself. And yet, throughout my life, I have hated and avoided criminality and dishonesty, searching to conduct business in as ethical a manner as possible.

Now I was staying with the three (very English, Etonian) boys I had met in Wales. They lived in a small castle, the older two went to Eton and their father drove an old Rolls Royce. They were kind to me, but clearly not sure how to take me. In Wales, they had had great respect for my knowledge of the mountains, the winds and the tides. But here? What did I know of Huntin', Shootin' and Fishin'? The shooting I knew was rabbits and wild duck to eat, not standing in a line while farm hands beat the brush to drive pheasants, quail and suchlike into a barrage of shots.

Our fishing was for urgent food and involved setting nets and nightlines, not standing in a river in thigh boots with a fishing rod and throwing back most of the fish. I had told them I was going to hitch-hike there and one of them had exclaimed that "I was jolly plucky", but I had no idea what he was talking about. I was not a peasant at dinner, I had been brought up to have manners and make polite conversation. I even enjoyed (and still do) being a chameleon – adapting to my environment as best I can.

I am happy to be an outsider, unaccepted when I worked as a labourer, unaccepted when I have dined with the Mighty. Of course 'unaccepted' is a far cry from 'ostracized'. I am not scandalous or outrageous. I have learned to fit in but I just don't feel like anyone else.

When it came time to leave my kind hosts, there was no longer any question of my hitch-hiking. I was put on a train and sent home in time for school.

My Welsh/English life was always a dichotomy in those days. I was accepted by neither. I was away from Wales in an English school for eight months a year. I could read and sing in Welsh, with a just passable accent, yet I spoke only a smattering of the language. I had a romantic leaning towards Wales as a land, the place in which I was brought up, but I also had the English superiority vis-à-vis the Welsh. As for the English, I saw them as rich and conventional. I did not mind the rich part, but I had been raised to despise conventionality. I had been convinced that convention and conformity are boring. I was not aware that some of these qualities actually make the World go round and put food on the table. They politely accepted me because I spoke the language of an educated person with the accent of a boy whose parents could afford to send him to a private school, but there was always something of the anarchist, the loner in me that troubled those wealthy English people with their bridge parties and chintz-covered furniture. No one knew quite what to make of me... I liked it that way, I still like it that way – no labels please.

XXI

COURTING DEATH ON CLIFFS

Also, in that summer of 1954 (when I was ten, my friend Alan, a year older) we had spent many days walking and scrambling up rock faces that deserved the respect of ropes. Neither of us had any formal rock-climbing instruction, but we knew enough not to use ropes if we did not know how to use them... as I came to learn, fatally:

A couple of years later, I was acting as guide to a cousin who wanted to climb Mount Snowdon by the Crib Goch saddle. One section, near the summit, involves a series of 'knife-edges', where ground on either side of the path falls away on either side to a precipice just a few feet away. Like crossing a rope suspension bridge in the jungle, one could have crossed over on all fours, but instead we walked, buffeted on either side by the ferocious updrafts of wind which swept dense cloud up to collide with the wind from the other side, bursting skywards like a vast mist geyser. The path would then swoop up again to another small peak where you could hold on to the rocks, before falling away again to another 'knife-edge'. On the way back down, we were already fearful of the approaching dusk (in the cloud and driving rain it was dark enough in broad daylight), when we passed two groups of three young men, roped together. Although I was still only about twelve years old, I summoned the courage to ask the leader if it was wise to be still going up with dusk not far off and the weather so dour. He brushed me aside, saying he was a trained instructor and knew what he was doing. My concern was that the two trios were walking fast while roped together, if one slipped, the other two would not have a stable position of purchase to hold him back. So that far from saving him, they themselves would be dragged over by him.

When we reached home, Father was listening to a radio report saying that the second trio was lost in the dark on the mountain. He called the police with my account of meeting the two groups – but in the morning, they were found dead at the bottom of a thousand-foot cliff. These mountains, which I looked upon as my playground or back yard, claimed (and claim to this day) many fatalities. I was brought up with many great natural dangers, and indeed courted them: between the tides and their currents, the craggy mountains with almost zero visibility in the clouds and vertical drops over cliffs on every side. Yet today's urban child faces just as many dangers from modern society: abduction, drug abuse, traffic accidents, bullying and firearms.

The very first time I climbed Snowdon, many years before, my older siblings woke me at midnight to leave. I remember stumbling into my shorts and sweater, pulling on my tennis shoes, rubbing Dubbin (Mink Oil in the States, a grease to waterproof boots) into my bare legs (on the assumption that it would keep my legs warmer and drier). I was thrilled to be included on this expedition with my older siblings; any misgivings of fear of the unknown, of heights or rain or cold simply never occurred to me. I must have fallen asleep in the Jeep on the way to the foot of the Watkins Path. Aroused again, we started up through a great forest of rhododendrons twenty feet high, they dripped large splats of the rainwater that was steadily pouring from the night sky. I walked behind someone, just doggedly putting one foot in front of the other. The jungle over, the path led up the side of a river gully. We could hear the crash and tumble of running water on our right. We did not use electric torches, so soon our eyes adjusted to the darkness and we could stumble along pretty well. The way became steeper and steeper until, after about two and a half hours, we reached the final climb. Here, the path had disappeared completely and I could only continue to follow the boots in front of me. At least I could not look down and see just how steep this part is, or that there is a precipice below which takes care of anyone who slips and falls. Had it been light, I might have been more afraid – I certainly was on subsequent trips, not that fear ever stopped me following this tricky path. Somehow, being fearful, 'being chicken', was simply not in the cards – as long as I have lived, I have not considered mere qualms as a reason to turn back. Unless a situation spelled real disaster, I would continue if I could. Clearly fear is part of the instinct for self-preservation, but if there is a reasonable hope of survival, then you press on.

Once at the summit, I slept again, this time under a rock, with someone's raincoat over me. I missed the dawn and its rising sun… but then, so did everyone else. We were in thick cloud under incessant rain. I sat fascinated by the way the rain water beaded on my dobbin-smeared bare legs – perhaps I should have been wearing blue woad, instead of clothes, as the Picts of yore (those ancient cousins of Scots – who together kept harassing the Roman conquerors) are supposed to have done. I tried to see the sunrise from the summit of Snowdon several other times thereafter… and never did succeed, despite conscientiously consulting the weather forecast beforehand. That first time, I was probably six or seven years old. If that sounds a little too young to be climbing a 1,085 meter peak (the highest in England and Wales), I can only say that I have been out-walked by six-year-old great-nephews several times since.

Some couch potatoes have asked me why there was this compulsion to climb mountains in all weathers… I can only think that Britain in those days was grey and middling: everything was Rationed, Restricted and Controlled, standing in queues was a national pastime, public areas were cold and forlorn, smelling of stale beer, cigarettes and urine – so to walk up mountains in the hope of seeing a fabulous view was as liberating as it is to see a raven riding the up-draughts at the crest of a great cliff. We may have been broke and hungry – but hiking the mountains was a huge expression of freedom.

* * *

Now with my new climbing partner of my own age, Alan, we were traversing a rock face much steeper than the angle of repose, yet not quite vertical. He was getting excited and competitive, moving too fast from one tiny foot or finger-hold to the next. Suddenly he slipped and disappeared from view over the steeper slope below us. When I managed to climb down to him, he had landed on a shelf covered in grass and looked unhurt. That was, until he raised one hand that he had been nursing and showed me that a sharp piece of rock had almost filleted off the ball of his thumb, the fleshy part just above the wrist.

He mocked me when I tried to take the situation in hand. He told me, from his training as a Boy Scout, that he must be suffering from shock and "would I please give him a cup of hot, sweet, strong tea to calm his nerves!" Instead, we walked down the mountain to the nearest and most competent grown-up I knew: Amabel, wife of the famous local architect and creator of Portmeirion, Clough Williams-Ellis. They lived in a big old stone house that twenty-one-year-old Clough had inherited from his family. At once he set about re-designing the gardens, orienting vistas down which to admire the surrounding mountains. Many years later, when he was in his seventies, the house was gutted by fire. Clough and Amabel escaped unharmed and, far from bemoaning their loss, Clough was thrilled: he said the insurance would pay for the renovation he had always dreamed of and already had the drawings to execute. He immediately summoned a trusted builder and started to put his old 'pipe-dreams' into reality the very next day, before the glowing embers of the fire had even died. He lived into his mid-nineties, but even then, was never an 'old man'. He dreamed, he designed, he had fantasies that he realised and he never seemed to slow down for old age or expediency.

Amabel published some fifty books in her lifetime. She was a solidly built old lady with wiry grey hair, who usually wore clothes of locally made tweeds. She was already in her eighties when a granddaughter ran away to an Ashram in the mountains of northern India. Since the young mystic was only on speaking terms with her grandmother, Amabel flew to India and went to the Ashram to bring her back. Once there, she enjoyed it so much herself that she stayed on for a few months. Then, in due course, the two women (divided by some sixty years in age) returned to England together! She had the admirable quality of treating children as equals, so I was hoping she would take us to the doctor in her car, for Alan to have his hand sewn up. She took one look at his hand and refused that suggestion. Instead, she made a poultice of some herbs and skilfully bound up his hand for him. She said a doctor would make a big scar with his stitches, better by far to let it heal naturally. Then she plied us with that essential: the hot, strong, sweet tea that my friend had asked for in the first place, right after his accident.

Amabel was a staunch atheist and enjoyed teasing Father about his Christian faith, a faith that appeared to grow as he aged. We used to go to the tiny Anglican church on top of the Ynys, called: Eglwys Llanfihangel-y-Treathau, or: the Church of Saint Michael of the Shores. Most local people went to chapel (Baptist, Methodist, Wesleyan, Congregationalist, and other Protestant Nonconformists), where the singing was vastly superior, but one of the requirements was often to be a teetotaller, so any backsliders who liked a pint from time to time, finished up in our church. In every small town in the hills, there were large, gloomy chapels for each separate sect – for they hoped to convert everyone else to come to their chapel. In the mid-nineteenth century, half of Britain was Non-conformist, yet now, most of those chapels have been abandoned or converted into houses or artists' studios.

Once, returning to the house after an outing, my Parents found three brothers from a nearby farm, sound asleep on the lawn, all dead drunk. Father was upset that they had used some of his best Burgundy to get sloshed, but nevertheless made them strong coffee, loaded them in the Jeep and dropped them off a mile from their own home, to walk off their binge. Of course he never told their chapel-going father... and they never dared come back for more.

The traveller Giraldus Cambrensis recounts in 1223, that in Wales groups of people sang "In several different tones at the same time, producing a surprisingly melodious sound." Perhaps the whole tradition of singing in harmony or parts comes originally from Wales. I remember the old vicar, the Reverend Morgan, who preached his sermons for an hour or more, starting out almost hesitatingly, feeling his way into an evangelistic stride, where his halting English became a sudden torrent of poetic Welsh rhythm and force... the 'hwyl' of Welsh preachers. I have no idea if he was speaking in Welsh or English. It did not matter, for his language flowed, it sang, the flood of the tide was upon him and within him, and surged forth in extemporaneous poetry with the ultimate solution of hellfire! Part song, part poetry and all inspired from above.

Miss Griffiths, the eternally ancient organist, played the harmonium or pump organ, pumping the air with her feet (of course, in those days there was no electricity in the church). Gradually the pumping became a little weaker until one day, she hurt herself badly by accidentally tying the laces of her high, lace-up boots together, so she took a bad fall. We only knew how well she played this harmonium, when my eldest sister was married in the church and asked a brilliant young organist who was up at Oxford with her, to play. He found there were only a couple of stops that worked and that it didn't work at all unless certain other stops were left open but not working. For her wedding, the music was even worse than under poor old Miss Griffiths!

There was one member of the congregation who "had been chapel" and now came to our little church. A very large, prosperous farmer, he sang a huge bass, in harmony, which filled the church. Mr Jones the Bacon, was also a church warden (as Father also became) and his very size and voice itself instilled Faith. I never learned why he no longer went to chapel.

Mr Jones had a son who was a particularly gifted singer, but too shy to perform for anyone else, even too shy to sing in church or chapel. A producer from the BBC asked Father if he might record someone local, singing as they went about their work. He asked Mr Jones about his son. "He'll never sing if he knows he's being recorded," said the farmer, "just come at 5.30 when he's doing the evening milking and pass around to the window of the dairy. You'll get your music all right." So, now picture three city gents in dark, three-piece suits and shiny shoes, crawling across the farmyard under the pouring rain, their knees deep in cow filth and mud, clutching the old-fashioned, bulky tape recorder and microphone! Who knows whatever happened to the tape recording? Was it ever aired on the radio? Did it disappear into the archives?

As it turned out, our afternoon with Amabel passed pleasantly in theological discussion washed down with more cups of tea and some home-made cake. She never gave the impression that she was trying to convert us but she did show her disdain for 'old-fashioned faith values'. I forget how I eventually got home, probably by hitchhiking. It was only about eight miles by road and in those days, most people would pick you up.

Back then, neither hitchers nor drivers were particularly concerned for their own safety. Everyone did it when necessary and those who did not stop their cars, either had a full load already or were just 'dogs in the manger' who didn't want a dirty stranger in their new cars. At nineteen, I made lifelong friends with a family who gave me a ride in Tarsus (eastern Turkey), where Saul had his revelation ("Saul, Saul, why persecutest thou me?") and became Paul, eventually Saint Paul. That family always found space in their car and enjoyed many such encounters. In their lives, they had offered hundreds of rides to strangers and even made real friends, such as myself. Expressways, the press and insurance companies have changed much of that. It is a much different world now, but then it was a very practical means of transport, by sharing a car going in the same direction. For me it was a way of life.

Once, I had gone to the dentist, dropped off by someone, or perhaps I had gone by train for a few stops. He pulled two molars "to make space for my wisdom teeth", and told me to go straight home and rest. Instead, I set off towards the mountains to go climbing by myself, as was my wont. I had walked a mile or so toward the hills and away from home, holding my thumb up for any of the few passing cars, when finally one pulled over for me… it was my dentist! "You live in the opposite direction, don't you? Is this how you go home and rest?" He asked, so I confessed that I was going climbing. He did not try to send me home, he seemed resigned to where I was bound and graciously dropped me off when our paths separated…

Yes, hitch-hiking seems to have gone the way of hallucinogens. It would seem that the baby-boomers who all did it when they were young, now fear for the lives of their children and themselves. Nowadays, only the very poor hitch, and few people pick them up. For myself, in the fifties and sixties, it served as a superb introduction to locals and locales, from Britain to the Persian Gulf (through Iran), from Mauritania to Egypt. I am afraid no one would pick me up now. There is an assumption that when you're old, you should be rich enough to buy a ticket on public transport or buy your own motorcar. Most of the people I pick up myself are only going half a mile and could have walked it. As for acid, people seem to prefer crack and cocaine to hallucinogens. That's the way it goes. The 'mind-expanding' drugs of the sixties have given way to addictive ones.

I was beginning to understand that one of my prerequisites for enjoying life was to choose what I did. There were givens, such as going to school and university (further education was assumed to be necessary). Manners were required and anyway, I quickly discovered how much more pleasant, agreeable and open life is, if approached with manners. I yearned for adventure.

I dreamed of travelling anywhere I wished to go, rather than where I was sent. Since I had no money, that meant I had to walk, so walk I would and Alan and I covered a good many miles together. When I could finally afford a real bicycle, as a teenager, I would set myself targets, usually fifty miles away. A round hundred miles in a day seemed like a good day's ride.

PART 2

THE JOURNEY

XXII

THE FLYING DUTCHMAN

In 1955, my Parents rented out our family house to a bishop for his family holiday for a month in the summer. Apparently, the arrangement annoyed Father so much that the lease included him in the house rental as a 'Landlord's Fixture'. He did not want to be kicked out of his own house, just when his work writing was going well (but my Parents were broke). In point of fact, like the rest of us, he made himself scarce before they arrived, for our family all dispersed in different directions. Father moved up into the mountains to the house that he and Mother had occupied when the Second World War was declared, the house where they were inundated with refugees for a while. Alan and I tried staying with him, but he was so absorbed in his work that however much we walked in the mountains, we felt in the way. We walked back to stay in the tiny, one-roomed cottage which was part of our property, a hundred yards from the main house and down on the rocky shore.

That tiny house had been the abode of old 'Johnny Flatfish'. He was long gone when we arrived in 1948, but his tale lived on. He had probably died before the War. It was a very small, one-room stone cottage with walls three feet thick and a sloping stone floor. There was a large chimney with open fireplace, upon which he must have done his cooking, just as we did. Of course there was no running water, no drains, no electricity or telephone. The highest of the spring tides came within feet of the front door and the cows from the neighbouring farm (old Mr Edwards) hung out at that door, like crowds trying to get into a popular nightclub. It was better they not manage to come in, since inside and out, they would leave ripe souvenirs of their visits.

Johnny had a double-jointed big toe. Local lore had it that he would stand out on the sands in the rising tide, a gunny sack over his shoulder and harpoon in his hand. He would wiggle his special toe vertically, to resemble a lug-worm coming up into the tide to feed. Of course the plaice would pounce, they had never seen such a huge lugworm, it would be a feast. Their gourmandizing was cut short by the spear of Johnny Flatfish and the next thing they knew was his gunny-sack full of their cousins.

Years before, when I was too young to be aware of what my older siblings were up to, they hatched a plan and pulled our Parents in to add a measure of 'authority'. They had decided that the poor children of rich parents who were forced to spend their summer holidays in the staid, fancy hotel of Portmeirion, across the estuary, must find the routine of dressing for dinner, long slow meals and above all, a schedule, appallingly boring. They must have been a little bored themselves to hatch such a plot, to kindly provide adventure for some unknown children whom they assumed would be bored!

They had painted a seductive poster (my eldest sister, the sailor, was a dab hand at painting mermaids) offering '24 hours of children's adventure'. The fine print stipulated that they must get their parents' approval by having them telephone our Parents. They were to leave with warm and waterproof clothes and expect to be blindfolded for some time. The first clue they were given, sent them to one of the last remaining anti-aircraft posts out in the estuary. There, another clue sent them to the top of a hill on our side of the estuary, but out of sight of our house. There, another clue sent them back down to the beach where they would find a cave with lanterns and matches ready to enter.

I was too young to participate, but as I remember it three children volunteered. Their parents spoke to our Parents and the plot was authorised. We watched them as they started to cross the estuary at low water. The instructions had told them where and when to do so. We watched as they found the next clue (nailed as promised to one of the anti-aircraft posts in the sand). From there on, I could not see them from the house, but apparently everything went as planned. My siblings, 'the gang', watched as they tried to open, light, and close the storm lanterns they had left. They were city children, not used to kerosene lamps, but finally they managed and went inside the cave.

I am claustrophobic and even when my brother took me there later, I hated the extremely narrow, diagonal cleft over a slab of rock, which led further on down to the body of the cave. Even as a child, it was close quarters and the last time I went in (at the age of eighteen) I had to let out all the air in my lungs to pass at one point.

Once they were down in the dripping, 'main hall' of the cave, where you had to lean on the slab of rock because you could not stand up straight, a kind girl's voice told them to blow out their lanterns and they would be rescued. The lights out, my older siblings (with precautionary kerchiefs as masks over their noses and mouths) slid down the rock and welcomed them in a medley of stage accents. They blind-folded the children and warned them not to try to escape. Then they helped them back up the great slab of rock and led them out of the cave, making sure they did not hit their heads on the very low ceiling.

Now that they could walk, their hands were bound and they were led to where our Father waited in the Jeep. He drove them up into the hills, down into valleys, choosing the most twisting circuitous routes possible, with fords and potholes and rough fields. Finally, they were brought to the old abode of 'Johnny Flatfish' where the one north-facing window (a small brass porthole from a ship) had been blacked out. Their blindfolds removed, they were forbidden to leave the cottage. They were given a sumptuous dinner with lots of hard cider and even some rationed chocolate and then, as the sun set, the porthole was unveiled for them to look out and see the expensive, uptight hotel where they were staying with their parents just a mile away, right opposite! They were asked if they would like to stay the night with my siblings, now that they knew where their parents were, and they all accepted with alacrity. My siblings entertained them with ghost stories and they all sang songs late into the night... They were delivered back to their families in the morning, dirty, tired and thrilled by the adventure.

Followers of the television series *The Prisoner* might be amused to learn that this little enactment of mystery took place some twenty years before the series was filmed at the hotel and on the very same estuary of the Traeth Bâch, where the mysterious Great White Ball of the surreal story, rolled around.

Well, this was where Alan and I decided to hang out for a while, but the cows had already managed to get in, so first we had to shovel out the cow-pats, then wash down the floor with buckets of sea water – which was closer to hand than the fresh water supply at the cow's trough. Father sometimes used the cottage to write in, when our house became too rowdy. There was a pine table and chair, a couple of collapsible army beds, even a chemical toilet, so that we need not join the cows. Outside the front door, there was a healthy growth of stinging nettles that can give you an itching rash for days afterwards, if you so much as touch the leaves. Unlike poison ivy, they can be cooked as soup, but when they are growing they can be vicious. Children soon learn their lesson and take care not to touch them, they also learn to find the broad-leafed dock plant that often grows alongside nettles and serves as a soothing antidote.

We started cooking on the big open fire, cooking things

that young boys cook: canned baked beans, eggs, bacon, sausages and baked potatoes. We bickered like an old couple and every day set out for a long walk in the hills or right up into the mountains. We could not use the boats; they went with the rental of the house.

Years later, a friend asked me in amazement, why I climbed the nearby mountains so assiduously? I replied, taking my cue from Sir Edmund Hillary of climbing Mount Everest: "Because they are there." Now I think of the painter Soulages who, when asked why he painted mostly in black, answered: "Because it exists". I know that is not a satisfactory answer. You can just look at black, you can just look at the mountains, you do not necessarily have to become intimately involved with them. Nevertheless, we all make choices of degrees of involvement. The nexus being: 'to be content to contemplate', or 'to actually participate and engage'. Again, the extreme penury of post-war Britain, the greyness, the poverty, the lack of hope, the similarity with Soviet Russia – with rationing over only in 1954 – made walking the mountains a huge expression of freedom, of choice, of joy. There might be very little food, but there was lots of dramatic scenery in which to wander.

On a clear day, the mountains stood out in all their minute detail, the major crags could be seen from twenty miles away, yet one knew there was a great deal undisclosed. It felt as if you could reach out and touch them. The mountains, temptresses that they are, lured one out to meet them. At that distance, it looked as if a few paces would scale their heights. Memories of aching legs and thirsty body were forgotten and the siren call of the hills would win out. Then, from their heights, you could be rewarded for your efforts with astonishingly distant views, back down to the family house, the green fields of the lowlands, the ocean scintillating in the sunshine. To this day, I love these mountains and they call to me every time I go back to visit.

On a cloudy day, visual memories were recalled – you

knew the hills were still there and the fact that one would be walking in a perpetual drizzle did not seem to matter – besides, sometimes the clouds would be suddenly torn open by the wind and there would be a quick snapshot, a cameo of a view, framed and circumscribed by cloud, even intensified because of that very frame created by the clouds, a flash that might disappear again within seconds, but remained inscribed upon the mind's eye. It was the sunny walks that I remember most vividly, but even the walks in the rain and fog left vivid memories, for there was something innately seductive about those crags, and yet, not everyone listened to the siren call. People came to stay and never ventured into the mountains – but we two boys gave in to it every day.

Most hikes were in the rain and mist. That was the simple law of averages. Those hikes led to introspection. One trudged on, watching the rugged ground in front of one's feet, automatically putting one foot in front of the other, thoughts turning in on themselves and the mind fertile. Whereas, on a clear, sunny day, the limitless view invited the mind to open wide with wonder, then the brain knew no boundaries. Thoughts flew and soared on the vast landscape and found no perch. After a clear day's hike, I would return exhausted but with a happy satisfaction, full of sights. After a wet walk in the clouds however, my memories might go no further than the water dripping from the tip of my nose and my eyebrows and the boggy ground where my next footstep would fall. There would be the stories and thoughts that had satisfied me during the day, but no joyful visual images.

At that point, I already knew that, in Wales, if you don't do something just because it's raining, you will never get anything done. So, many hikes were very wet, though in the summer, there were frequent droughts and hiking could become a hot and thirsty proposition.

One clear night, we came back to our tiny cottage, just as night had fallen and a spring tide was rising. It was dark, but the moon had already risen. We had not even lit any candles indoors yet so our eyes were attuned to the blackness – looking out at the tide, we saw the silhouette of a sailing dinghy floating by with no sails hoisted. Ghostly in the moonlight on the calm rising tide, she was drifting by. I hurriedly grabbed a rubber flashlight and suggested to Alan that we swim out to the dinghy and see what had happened, why it was drifting. He did not like the idea, so I stripped and started swimming out alone. Naturally, he called after me that it was "Probably a ghost ship, full of dead seamen who had died of thirst and scurvy". As I swam with the flashlight in my teeth, I was fully convinced that Alan was right and a horrible sight awaited me in the boat. Yet I carried on stubbornly. I could not change my plans now. It would show that I believed Alan's silly scary tales.

To this day, I have searched my memory for real fear, something stronger than a mild, cautionary apprehension, and found none. It was not like filling the coalscuttle at night, when I would indeed be frightened. It was an automatic reflex to swim out to the drifting boat in the dark. It needed to be done, just as my eldest sister leapt overboard and dived under the boat to push the centreboard up again, just as Father jumped overboard to disentangle the boat from his fishing nets. So I knew that I just had to make a real attempt at saving the boat. If I failed, then I had failed, but at least it would not have been for want of trying. Had it been a rough and stormy night, I would certainly have thought twice before attempting the rescue, but it was a still, clear night with a mammoth tide, so I just did it.

As I approached the floating black shadow, etched from behind by the moonlight on the water, I thought of the moment when I would grab the gunwale and haul myself up to look inside: there might indeed be dead bodies on the floorboards. Perhaps there would be dead seamen, frozen slouched over their oars, their skin burned black to blisters, their tongues swollen with thirst. Nevertheless, I reached up and grabbed the gunwale and pulled myself up. I peered over the edge to see the dead people inside and shine my torch on their tortured frames. It was a perfectly normal, empty boat – a 'Flying Dutchman', no less – I had admired this 20-foot class of international racing dinghy from afar. It was so much more efficient, fast and sophisticated than anything we had to sail at home. In a moment, I was over the gunwale and into the boat – once there, I discovered that it had been anchored on only five feet of rope! As mentioned before, the vertical rise and fall of spring tides could be as much as 34 feet. It must have been abandoned on a sand bank on an ebb tide and with so little line on the anchor, the next rising tide lifted her free, along with her anchor – and up the estuary she drifted. The stupidity of leaving her on too short a line aston- ished me and in moments I had freed the anchor rope from its cleat and paid out enough line to catch the anchor properly where I was. I felt it grab, tugged it to test its hold and belayed it to its cleat.

I swam ashore again and tried to irritate Alan with "He was too scared to swim out and save the boat" – he responded with a mature: "Someone had to light the fire and start cooking dinner, while you were messing around out there. Now what are you going to do?" The irony that it was a Flying Dutchman Class that had washed up and the ghost legend of the Flying Dutchman, was not lost on us.

Next morning, before the tide rose again, I went out to admire my catch. She was lying on the sea grass, in a bed of rose sea-pinks, buzzing with honeybees which only sting when you tread on them. Poor things, we often got our bare feet stung and pulling out the bee's barb disembowelled them, so they died. It was not their fault if we clumsily trod on them, and it was very painful – I seem to remember that we followed up with an intense blue dye that we used to tint the whitewash for the outside of the house – I suppose the dye was alkaline and relieved the pain. This time I was careful where I set my bare feet and was not stung.

XXIII

THE JOURNEY BEGINS

Now that we had the wherewithal to travel, five whole pounds of it, we packed our rucksacks and set out to walk back to the house where Father was holed-up to write. It was about fifteen miles over the mountains, around the head of 'our' estuary and across the head of its twin – the one that had been reclaimed as farmland in the early nineteenth century.

As we set out, we must have looked like Hobbits, with our small, boyish statures and large rucksacks, but at that moment, we felt more like Tolkien's Aragorn, the Strider. We were well rested, the day was bright and a great trek lay ahead of us so there was purpose in our strides. True, after a few miles in the heat of the day, we really would be again reduced to Hobbits: tired, short-legged folk, out of their depth on a long journey, but nevertheless stubbornly trudging on.

We were two little boys in shorts. As we plodded ahead, sights evoked stories from the past but once we were in unfamiliar country (on our third day), my memory kept itself busy with all the miscellaneous thoughts that tumble higgledy piggledy out of the dusty, disorganised attic of my mind.

I had only one pair of long trousers that I had inherited. They were chequered and my family had dubbed them my 'Newmarket Bags' – Newmarket being one of the most famous horse racecourses in England, with many shady 'bookies' or illegal betting agents who wore flashy clothes, hence Newmarket Bags. So of course we wore shorts. We had no sophisticated all-weather gear, 'Gortex' didn't exist and whatever was available for the Everest expedition (no doubt 'oilskins') was not available because of clothes rationing – not to mention price. I had a cheap plastic mackintosh which I had shortened so it would not get in the way of my legs and stuck the hem to the collar with paper glue to make a hood – of course it fell off the first time I used it. There was no plastic glue around. As for our footwear, Alan had a pair of real leather boots because his father said that his feet had stopped growing, so it was worth buying good ones. I wore high-top plimsolls with very thin soles. I wonder if they were invented by Samuel Plimsoll, who perfected the Plimsoll Line – that you may see on the side of every commercial vessel. It shows the safe water line of a laden ship in waters of varying salinities.

One of Father's secretaries was called Miss Plimsoll, and she assured us that it was indeed her great grandfather who had invented 'the line'. I wish I had asked her about the shoes as well, I do seem to remember that she was fleet of foot. By then they were manufactured by Dunlop and were also called 'daps' (Dunlop Athletic Shoes) – but to me they were 'plims'. I must have walked and climbed through quite a few pairs.

It was many years before Father hired a year-round secretary to take care of the business side of being an author, so he took to hiring a secretary for a short period each year. There was a woman who came from London and stayed at our house. The first morning, he showed her to her small office where a year's unopened mail awaited her attention. He asked her to open every envelope and sort it all out, making a list of questions for him to answer. When she did not come down for lunch, he went in search of her and found her crumpled over the desk in tears. There was not a single letter in sight – she had burned the lot in the boiler in the kitchen! The very sight of a year's mail had been too much for her... he used to say that it took him ten years to sort out the problems created by all that unanswered mail.

Then there was Mr Bigger. He had been Father's secretary at the Admiralty during the War. He lodged with two spinster sisters in the village, rare birds in that they were Catholics. There were very few Catholics in Wales, where non-conformist chapels and the Anglican Church covered the spiritual needs of most people.

Mr Bigger was a flabby, mild-mannered little man and he would have to walk over the hill to our house to work every day – perhaps three-quarters of a mile. The first morning he did not arrive. Mother suggested that the walk was too far. Father pointed out that during the War he had walked to work and back, several miles, all the time that there were no buses at all, for want of petrol and drivers. Eventually Mr Bigger telephoned from the village to say that the geese at old Mr Edward's little farm would not let him by... we all thought that hilarious. Even I (the smallest) knew that if you charged a hissing, threatening goose, it would turn and run. But Mr Bigger was a city man and very much a secretary at that. From then on, he had to take the long way round, by road and then up our rocky driveway. There were no geese loose at the larger farm on the hilltop.

As an extreme counterpoint to Mr Bigger, there was Candida, the daughter of John Betjeman (the poet and crusader for the preservation of Victorian architectural buildings). She was a quite different kind of secretary: a blond Bardot bombshell before Bardot made the scene. She was in such awe of Father (what had Betjeman told her?) that she wore silk miniskirt suits of the most brilliant colours that she had bought specially to come and work for Father. She fitted into our crazy lifestyle by being barefoot all the time, but she still wore the tight little silk suits to go sailing. If she was impressed by Father, I was doubly impressed by her...

Alan and I walked half over, half around, the small hill behind the house, following a tiny path created more by sheep than by man – the very path attempted by Mr Bigger a few years before. The hill was overgrown with gorse bushes, their dark green thorns a strict warning to keep our distance, their deep yellow flowers a brilliant contrast to the green. In between the gorse there were bare rocks and patches of short grass, grazed by hardy little Welsh sheep that had left wisps of their wool on the gorse thorns. In other places the hill was covered in bracken, a wild fern that overgrows the grass. In those days, farmers burned it or cut it for use as bedding for their cattle, but nowadays its smoke is considered carcinogenic and such practices are illegal. When young, bracken closely resembles fiddleheads, but as far as I know, it was never eaten. In the autumn, it goes an orange brown, so whole hillsides look as if they are aflame.

We went through an old iron kissing-gate (devised by farmers to withstand sheep) and looked down into a little barrel-shaped glen that led down to the tidal beach. The small valley was shaded with a few old oak trees that leaned in towards each other from the sides, almost meeting at the top. In the eighteenth century, ships were built here, as the natural shape of the narrow valley allowed men to work up the side of the ship without much (if any) scaffolding. When I was younger, perhaps still at the harness age, Mother took us on picnics there in the shade of the oaks. She loved to sketch the gnarled old trees in pastels, no doubt the offspring of the original oaks used to build the boats in days gone by. The place had a whiff of magic to my young mind, a place associated with elves, fairies and goblins.

Now we bounced down into the valley and up the other side, then skirted a couple of hay fields, keeping strictly to the sides so as not to trample the crop. There were foxgloves growing along the edges of the fields, their tall stalks hung with purple trumpets the size of fingers – hence the name 'digitalis'. As children we had been warned about how poisonous they are, but that never seemed to stop us from wearing them on all ten fingers – and probably sucking those fingers afterwards. The morning was already warm and a skylark hovered high against the blue sky, as if held up by its own frenetic song, rather than constantly beating wings – invisible from such a distance.

We passed the little grey church – Eglwys Llanfihangel-y-Traethau – with its walled cemetery grown with tall yew trees. There I had dozed through many an interminable sermon. Near the west door stood a strange vertical gravestone, about five feet high and roughly square (8 inches or so to each side). It was engraved with letters – just recently deciphered by an archaeologist friend – in abbreviated Latin and mostly Roman characters. It was a tombstone from the twelfth century and read: "Here is the grave of Wledr, Mother of Hoedliw who first built this Church in the time of Owain Gwynedd." King Owain ruled Gwynedd from 1137 to 1170, so the walls of the Church are some 150 years older than those of nearby Harlech Castle's Norman masonry.

The church itself had been rebuilt and repaired so many times over the centuries, it now looked like a non-descript little chapel, built in the nineteenth century, its very ancient origins covered over with pebble-dash and plaster.

We went down the lane between high stone walls, from the church and past the large, square rectory (forever dour beneath its great dark pine trees) it was said that a man, jilted at the altar, had hung himself from the great old, gnarled oak tree. That was where my brother had fallen over a sleeping cow as he ran down the lane in the dark of night on his way to catch an early train, giving him quite a fright since he was just thinking of the jilted suicide at the time. From there we carried on down the hill to the hamlet know as Ynys (pronounced 'un-iss'), which means 'island' in Welsh.

From the small sprinkling of cottages, the road runs across flat land that had been sea when Harlech Castle was built over seven hundred years ago. When my namesake Owain Glyn Dwr (the renowned Welsh Nationalist-separatist hero and 'guerrilla' – Father even claimed he was an ancestor) captured (in 1404) and held the castle for four years, it was still on a tidal sea and remained so until 150 years ago. Now it is rather marshy farmland. After half a mile we crossed the railway line at Ty Gwyn Halt, the one with a platform long enough for one door of the local train, where benighted passengers had thought it was the End of the World when they alighted in the dark only to find themselves surrounded by seawater from the great tidal wave. After that flat land, we walked up into the ancient highlands of the geological Harlech Dome. We trudged up a pretty lane which followed a small cascading river in its narrow valley, heavily wooded with 300-year-old oak trees with their very dark green canopy of leaves and lush green, moss-covered rocks below, where jagged edges of splintered rock were wrapped and cushioned by a velvet carpet of moss. The trees were clad with lichen, but only on their north sides. In this dark shade, the air smelled cool and fresh. The great roots of trees writhed, clutching piles of river rocks to their wooden embrace. The small river tumbled white and foaming down to its more peaceful way on the flat land, on down to the ocean. Bright rays of sunshine sparkled here and there, where beams of light found a path through the heavy foliage.

We walked past the tiny one-room cottage that Father had rented as his first house in Wales – when he was sixteen. It had been built as the first school in Meirionnydd. Now it was overgrown with trees. Just as it had been when he first rented it, there was still a small spring that came up in front of the hearth and ran across the floor and out of the door. He had kept his food in red and white spotted handkerchiefs, their corners tied together and hung from nails in the low rafters – out of reach of the rats. His annual rent had been two pounds, four days work on the farm and two pounds of honey – the cash had come out of his school pocket money. In those days, he thought little of walking from his school in Surrey to North Wales.

From there we followed a track down the bottom of a hanging valley, known locally as a *cwm*. This valley was wooded with oak, with some green fields surrounded by great dry-stone walls. Now another stream ran alongside us. The track led us past a small lake full of water lilies, a lush contrast to the barren landscape above, into which we were about to climb. We climbed up to an ancient, lonely church on a hill, where a service was held only once or twice a year. The view from the graveyard is spectacular and panoramic, so we stopped a few moments to take it in.

Our progress was much as it had been the year before, when my sister and I were riding the ponies – except that we did not have to stop to be shod at the blacksmith's, nor did we stop to graze, just to catch our breath and drink deeply from the rivulets that, despite the drought, still tinkled out of the bogs. But there was this vast difference: I had chosen this expedition, I had financed it, if I suffered it was my choice. Again, we had a hot, sunny day, too hot for comfort. I remember the toil of climbing steep slopes with my knapsack, the drudgery of putting one foot in front of the other, an automatic movement that somehow invoked the image that I was an overloaded truck with a 16-speed gearbox with which I was for ever 'changing' gears up and down. On this ancient road, we were above the tree line. The way was surely chosen to be in open country where brigands and highwaymen could not easily hide. Nowadays, law and the welfare state had put such dangers behind – but the view from up here was spectacular.

We looked down over the flat land that had been sea, the land across which we had just walked. We looked over to the hill behind my home, the Ynys, and we could see how it had been an island, all it took was to replace the wet green fields in our mind's eye with tidal sea water – for the fields were as flat as any water ever was. We could not see the house; the hill hid it from this angle. South and west of Ynys was the great sweep of depositional sand that holds Cardigan Bay in its arc – the beaches ironing out the irregular, jagged interjections of rock from the ancient mountain formations. As for the Bay itself, it was the beginning of the open ocean, the beginning of the outside world, beyond Britain and all that Britain meant. Over the horizon was Ireland, some say that you can even see it on a clear day, though I never saw more than haze upon the curved horizon.

By the same token, a seventeenth-century traveller who climbed Snowdon, claimed that you could see the whole of the British Isles and the coast of France – in which case, either the mountain was higher or the world flatter in his day – clearly he did not think there was much risk of anyone else being so foolish as to climb that peak again to verify his information... then again, perhaps he was merely practicing 'poetic licence'.

We picked up the same Roman Road I had taken the year before with my sister on horseback. Here we were above the tree line, the moors dried out and burned by the long drought. While the bogs in lower ground were still waterlogged and bright green, up here the still air smelled of dried herbs and parched heather. The usual wayside foxgloves and nettles could not survive up here. The vegetation was stunted, with wind-whipped heather, short reeds in wet boggy hollows, even a little bracken here and there. Our packs were minimal, but all the same they felt like lead: I carried my sleeping bag and most of the food, while Alan carried his own sleeping bag, a tiny camping gas stove and a small pup tent, of which he was very proud. We carried little water, knowing that there would always be a mountain stream wherever we went. It was years later that we all learned of fatal diseases from sheep manure or carcasses that make those crystal-clear mountain streams potentially lethal. Meanwhile, we enjoyed them in happy ignorance.

We passed Llyn Tecwyn Uchaf, a reservoir for some newer houses below. There were some ruined houses higher up, roofless, door-less, windowless shells built like the stone walls, of big stones and boulders – mostly without any mortar in-between. The highlands of Wales are dotted with these skeletons, once lived in as upland farms (no longer profitable or desirable) or groups of them where miners and quarrymen used to live during the week, then hurry down to their families and homes on the lowland for a square meal and chapel on Sundays… and who knows, perhaps a spot of beer (well, it was beer or chapel, not both – not worth the scolding from the Minister in front of everyone) and even some slap and tickle beforehand on the Saturday night?

From the reservoir, we plunged downhill into a recently planted government re-forestation project of fast-growing conifers for paper pulp and other junk uses. The bureaucrats had no use for slow growing oak, ash or beech trees. These single-species plantings were much maligned locally as prone to disease, not ecological, unnatural and ugly. Right now, the trees were not much taller than ourselves, yet already so deep green that they were dark and foreboding. We still walked on grass but soon, without sunlight, the growing trees would blanket the ground in needles and there would be no grass, no flowers, no heather. Evergreens seemed indeed like a deathly blight on the landscape.

At the head of the valley of the Dwyryd (which lower down became 'our' estuary), we came down through real deciduous woods again and briefly trudged the road to use the bridge at Maentwrog to cross the river, just as I had done on horseback. There is a single track toll bridge much lower down the river and had we been hitch hiking, that would have been the shortest, quickest way to go. Now however, we were determined to avoid walking on roads as much as possible. Besides, this longer way round was much more beautiful. So from this old stone bridge, we walked back up through more great oak woods, but this time with a heavy undergrowth of wild rhododendrons, and again out onto the open highlands to pick up the ancient track again. This time, we were further from the highest point, for here the Harlech Dome is replaced by the younger, more recently bent and folded mountains of Snowdonia. We skirted the flanks of Moelwyn Bâch – where, higher up, Alan had almost been killed, that time when he slipped on a cliff we were traversing. Amabel's magic herbs had by now totally healed his injured thumb. Now the view to the left was southwest down the larger valley of the Glaslyn, which had been dammed with the Cobb and reclaimed as farmland. The foothills still seemed to end in the flat sea, but in fact it was a green sea of grass crisscrossed by banks with hedges on top and ditches to drain the low-lying fields. Down there, it was an oasis beyond stone wall country which was everywhere else on higher ground. Down there, drainage was the issue. Up on the hills, stones were the issue. The stone walls were built to clear the surface of the fields so that grass would have a little more space to grow, besides defining property lines.

Oh yes! This view was my view. This was the landscape that I had chosen to wander and admire. The visibility was no clearer today than it had been when I passed this way on horseback the year before... but now it sang! From now on, I hoped that I would choose my views, whether they be of a slag heap outside Essen (Ruhr) one foggy, freezing December night or the brilliant bird's-egg blue of enamel on the Shah (or Imam) Mosque in Esfahan, the windows of the Sistine Chapel as the sun sets behind them and a chamber orchestra plays Vivaldi's *Four Seasons*, the dirt-floored, filthy house of a crack-head in the Mexican desert. To each view I say: "Seize this view, for this I may never see again." It took cancer, forty years later, to see just how truly fundamental is that thought. "We are on Earth but for a brief span of time, if we lose our lust for life, we lose our lives."

We passed the sharp little point of Craig Ysgafn and then over the rounded flanks of Moelwyn Mawr, a particularly round, grassy mountain with few sharp rocks visible. Below its surface it is honey-combed with old slate mines that were used to store artworks in, from the major museums of London during the War. It is still a mystery to me how they kept them dry, for whenever I had gone inside those mines, water poured, rather than dripped, from the roof and ran down the floors where there had once been narrow gauge tracks for slate wagons. We came down into the *cwm* between Moelwyn Mawr and the next mountain Cnicht, totally different from the Moelwyns. It looked like the Matterhorn, or a dinosaur lying on its belly with its scaly back the long sharp ridge of rocks.

I used to enjoy walking up the 'dinosaur's back' to the summit and then, rather than retrace my steps, would continue a short way down the other side, before turning right and scrambling down a 'chimney' or narrow cleft in the vertical rocks. At the bottom of this cleft was a perfect scree slope, stone debris broken off from the cliff above, lying at 43° – the angle of repose. You could run and jump down this slope, the stones sliding under your feet as you landed, absorbing the shock and hastening your descent. Scree-riding is a summer form of skiing, but it is best done on rarely travelled slopes because each passer-by reduces the angle of the slope a little until the stones will no longer slide under your feet. It is not for the faint-hearted and you have to keep concentrating on your next landing place, for if you hit a solid, stationary rock you are likely to break a leg.

It is always easier going up mountains formed by glaciers, than down them. This is because the rounded, armchair-shaped valley known as a *cwm* or *cirque* frequently drops away into nothing at its bottom end (where the giant's legs would be if one were sitting in the cwm). They are cut off by a transverse glacier lower down. There are often lazy, meandering 'mature' streams in these high up, hanging valleys, which suddenly turn into wild, tumbling torrents when they reach the end of the valley. Climbing up to such a hanging valley is clear walking, you can see how steep it will get ahead and skirt the vertical parts. Going down, on the other hand (especially in cloud or in the dark), the way may seem almost flat, but when you reach the end of the valley, there is no way to tell where it leads to a vertical drop and where a descent may be negotiated without breaking one's neck.

As I had leapt and slid down this rock-strewn slope, I thought of a story Father had told of when he was a boy, climbing Cader Idris near Dolgellau and meeting a shepherd looking for a lamb on a scree slope. The old man said to him: "Come along with me, young gentleman, I'll show you something you've never seen before." Father followed him to a spot where a mountaineer had missed his footing while scree-riding, tripped on a large rock sticking up through the loose stones and fell forward with full force and cracked his skull on another rock. The shepherd asked. "See where his brains come out all over those stones?" Father pocketed a small one with plenty of blood on it, though he was less sure of the brains, and kept it in his 'museum' – a child's collection which disappeared over the years. So I never did see the bloody, brain-splattered stone, though the story remained engraved on my mind, as if the dangers of scree-riding were not already sufficiently obvious to keep all of my attention.

Looking up at these relatively parched mountains, there were still a few boggy patches where water pools in rock depressions and the grass and stubborn little reeds there keep their emerald colour despite the drought. There were no other hikers to be seen. Everyone climbs Snowdon, but many ignore its remarkable minor cousins. There were white spots here and there; if they moved they were sheep, if they were stationary they were mushrooms (scale at this distance is difficult to gauge), but with the present drought, there were no mushrooms. Sometimes, if we were really lucky – and on this trip we were not – the white spots could be a herd of wild goats. These goats are superb. Their hair (neither fur nor fleece) is long and hangs down half way to the ground, especially when groomed. Not that they are ever groomed in nature. The bucks sport great horns as long as 45 cms, which sweep back in a proud arc. I was told that a few individuals are sometimes caught by professional rugby players to serve as mascots for the Royal Welsh Fusiliers. A herd is corralled into a narrow valley trap, and there a few are tackled like the opponent team in a rugby match. Alas, they do not last long in the stressful life of London, with their horns polished and their hair shampooed and groomed into silver tresses. Life on the parade ground is not worth living when compared to life on the cliffs of Snowdonia.

From where we were, the nearest visible house was half a dozen miles away, down on the coast. Closer by, the next village was hidden below in a valley. Our feeling of isolation was exhilarating: we were alone and capable. We could keep on walking until we could walk no more and camped. The independence we felt was thrilling. We were proud of our strong little legs.

Where our track reached its lowest point in the valley was the tiny hamlet of Croesor with a shop-cum-post office, chapel and primary school, all built of slate. For fencing, slate was taken from rejected slabs up to 2m long and 60 to 90cm wide, which were slightly buried at one end (the earth was so shallow over the rocks below, it was impossible to bury them deeper) and then held together with the next piece by means of heavy twisted wire. In those days, where the slabs of slate had fallen down or where a gate was needed, farmers used Victorian iron bedstead ends to fill the gaps. This curious stop-gap solution had led an uncle who farmed a rich success-ful farm in the west of England to ask Father: "… if the farmers slept on gates, since their bedsteads were already used as gates?" Later, with the mode for gentrification, antique shop owners came all the way from London. They bought the bed ends for a song and had them restored, to sell to a new generation of Yuppies moving into renovated slum houses in London. Sometimes they even stole them when the farmer was not around, leaving a gaping hole in the fence.

At Croesor, we turned left and walked down the lane wide enough for one vehicle at a time, the last half mile to Parc, the sixteenth-century house where Father was writing. It was late afternoon, though the summer sun would not set for a few hours yet. Alan and I were hot, thirsty and hungry, but we knew very well that there was no such thing as a refrigerator to raid in this house. As in our family house, there was no electricity (not to mention that this house still had no drains or running water either). Food was still scarce and scarcer still when Father was the caterer.

He was sitting in the big dark kitchen, hunched, bear-like (menacingly or protectively?) over his little Olivetti 22 typewriter, hardly any larger or heavier than a modern laptop – an invention he would have loved to work on, had he lived another thirty years. His big hands were pounding away fast with four fingers, interspersed with long periods of silent reflection. The fire was smouldering in the huge fireplace (where one brother had "cleaved his sibling in twain with an axe"). He was a little confused to be interrupted by us, thinking he had just got rid of us ten days before, but he seemed not so displeased either. And so ended our first long day's trek.

Once we had slaked our thirst, we set about collecting wood and reviving the fire, knowing that this was the first step towards dinner. By then, he had put away his typewriter and marshalled his typescript into a neat pile. He poured himself a glass of wine and started making a very hot curry with cooked cold lamb and vegetables. I told him of our plan to walk to Bardsey Island. Far from saying we were too young to be travelling so far alone, the idea seemed to light his fire.

XXIV

THE JOURNEY BLESSED

Father, a notoriously meticulous writer, was never noted for his speed (whether writing, gardening or cooking – it was only the immediate urgency of sailing that got him really moving), but the setting sun still shone in through the big stone-mullioned window over the dining table in the kitchen when we finally sat down to his highly-spiced curry, complete with rice, pappadom, mango and lime chutneys and his favourite: Bombay Duck – dried and somewhat putrid small fish which are normally baked, but which, for want of an oven, we had toasted. They are illegal in the U.S. on grounds of food hygiene, but could also be illegal on the grounds of odour. All these delicacies, he must have brought from London. I never knew him to make a curry when Mother was around, so it was a personal indulgence. We ate everything with enthusiasm and burped rotten fish all night.

While he was still cooking, I recounted the story of saving the 'Flying Dutchman' and how I had been paid five whole pounds for it. That was when he told me that I had been robbed, for I was entitled (under the International Laws of Salvage) to one third of the value of the vessel, probably a few hundred pounds. He made me feel stupid and naïve but I am quite sure that in my shoes, he would have accepted nothing at all. I had only accepted the £5 because the owner insisted so forcefully and as Father pointed out, he had every reason to insist: because once I had accepted the £5, I could no longer make further claims of salvage rights! I've never had the opportunity to salvage another vessel so that knowledge has not advanced me one whit.

As we sat down to table, he came to sit at the head, bearing an Ordnance Survey 1 inch/mile map and another bottle of wine. Suddenly he was all enthusiasm, saying: "Well, of course you could follow the Path of the Saints: the twenty thousand saints who are buried on Bardsey Island after their pilgrimages there. Even the Great Wizard Merlin is said to be among them, but he's been 'buried' in a dozen places that I know of. Did you know that three pilgrimages to Bardsey used to be worth a pilgrimage to Jerusalem, or was it just to Rome? I forget. Did you know that 'Bardsey' (or Ynys Enlli, in Welsh) was also called 'Island of the Saints' – besides 'Island of Birds' and 'Island of Currents'?" At this point, he spread out the map, pushing the dinner things to one side. "If you go straight from here north to Clynnog where Saint Beuno is buried, then follow the north coast of the Lleyn Peninsula down here… to Aberdaron – that's where they might have found passage to Bardsey, so I expect you still can [it was only 1400 years later in history]. There's nowhere else you could get a boat to take you. Then, when you get there, you will see the remains of the abbey. There's a lighthouse there too – I forget the timing of its flashes – but it's an essential light when you're sailing round the point of the Lleyn up to the Menai Straits between Anglesey and the mainland. The tides run hard further out into the Irish Channel, so you want to keep in close to the coast, but that point there is very rocky, so you won't want to come in too close." He became so animated, it was as if suddenly he was back in his sailing boat with bare feet, instead of slippers – his old-fashioned climbing boots still had nails on the soles and jagged incisor teeth on the toes and heels. If you walked on a slate floor in them, you could slip up as if on ice (not to mention scratching up the floor). Now they sat waiting patiently for him by the front door: like old dogs hoping to go for a walk.

With that, we had Father's blessing – not that it would have occurred to me that anyone might think it a bad idea. I wasn't brought up to think that doing anything adventurous was a bad idea… short of some suicidal folly.

Alan and I washed the dishes as best we could in cold water, by the light of a guttering candle and staggered off to bed up the stone stairs. The treads were so worn by 400 years of feet that the risers hardly existed in the centre. To the sides, where the risers still stood, bright green moss grew on them year round, even during hot summer spells, such as the present one.

We slept in the bedroom above the kitchen, the one where smoke sometimes seeped up through the floorboards, and could be mistaken for the 'real' ghosts that pervaded the house. It was somewhat warmer there than in the master bedroom (where Father slept anyway), whose bed (in my experience) never dried more than to a heavy dankness. The next stage would be outright dampness, its usual state.

The 'priest holes', I had been told, were to hide Catholic priests during the Reformation, but I have since learned that, while they may sometimes have been used for such a purpose, they were originally put into large houses as safes in which to hide valued pewter ware and any silver they might own (which was little in the sixteenth century – the vast silver resources of Latin America were not yet fully exploited).

The ghosts came from stories of the violence and shame of past occupants. As a matter of fact, the family that built this house named 'Parc', was so wealthy, educated and informed, that the master of the house had a standing order with a bookseller in London, to send him every new play by Mr. Shakespeare, as soon as it was published.

One story told about Parc related to two brothers, tenant farmers, who lived there alone, farming the rough, highland fields around. One was perhaps not strong and certainly lazy. He did the accounts and a spot of cooking, but it was his brother who worked from before dawn to after dusk, trying to eke a living out of the poor soil and hazardous grazing. One night, he came home in the dark to see his brother leaning over the cauldron hanging above the fire. On a table, stood a candle and their account ledger. One glance at the accounts was enough to tell him they were bankrupt. Mad with rage at his lazy brother, he took up the great axe used for splitting wood and cleaved his weak brother in two, as he stirred the stew... then he hanged himself in remorse – from the kettle chain, that one right there, in the fireplace.

There were other stories, of young people disappointed in love and so on, but Mother was told one, when she was alone there one night. It was soon after my Parents' marriage and she had two wolfhounds with her at the time. Father had announced that he felt he should go and sit with an old neighbour who was dying and alone. He promised he would be back by morning, whether the neighbour died or not.

On the way down the valley to the dying man, he met another neighbour who lived further up the valley. He asked him if he would mind looking in on Mother, who was alone. "Perhaps you could chop a little wood for her?" He suggested. Well, the neighbour promised he would and indeed soon knocked at the door.

Mother invited him in and gladly accepted his company for a while. She accepted his offer to split some wood. But each time he came in with another armful, he would say things like: "So you're all alone in the Parc, by yourself, indeed. You couldn't pay me to spend an hour alone at night here." The wolfhounds were uneasy and kept pacing around (who knows if they had any kind of bedding to sleep on? Wolfhounds are skinny and hate sleeping on hard, cold, stone floors).

Finally, she had made him a cup of tea and he accepted it in front of the crackling fire: "Ever seen the legs of the fellow who chopped his brother in half with an axe? They say he hung himself in shame from this very kettle chain here." No, Mother said she hadn't seen the legs yet.

Then he continued: "Mind you, they say there's a great treasure buried here just below on the terraces where the orchard used to be in my granddaddy's day. They say that if you strike the lintel of this house with steel, at midnight, if you are the chosen one, a white dog will lead you to the treasure and start digging for you. But there again, they say that if you are not the chosen one, two great black dogs with fire in their eyes will hunt you over the mountains until you fall from a cliff and die. The ravens will find you in the morning...

"Well Missus, I'll be going. But no, you would never ever get me to stay here by myself alone. Not me. Well good night, Missus..." and he was gone in the dark.

As a teenager, I later regaled a small barbeque party, in this same house, with some of these tales. One guest, brought by neighbouring friends, burned his hand cooking hotdogs and listening to the stories at the same time... It was Mick Jagger – he still had a country accent, but the Stones were already making quite a name for themselves. The stories that we enjoyed so much together were not such fun for my young Mother, all alone and with no one to go to for company.

XXV

INTO THE WILD

In the morning, we both overslept and I was shocked when Father carried me out from my bed and dropped me in the 'laundry', a slate-lined pond in front of the house with steps down to the water where a spring came out – the water source for the house. We no longer used it as a laundry, since we used the water to drink. The spring water was an icy shock, but less of a shock than his playful gesture and above all, the human contact with Father, who had not carried me since I was an infant...

Confused by such intimacy and playfulness, I helped Alan to pack up. Somehow, I had become accustomed to the fact that once we are no longer infants, parents do not touch their children. They send their children away to school to be chastised with corporal punishment. Strangers, teachers were hired to touch them with brutal strokes of the cane, lash or whip. Parents don't touch their children – for fear that they become 'soft' or perhaps develop an Oedipus Complex? And here was Father actually carrying me outside to dunk me in icy water! It was not the icy water that shocked me but the warm grasp of his strong arms holding me.

The next time I remember touching him was some twenty-two years later, when I came to spend time with him as he died. I took his hand, huge but feeble by then. In those twenty-two years, there had been occasions, such as when I returned, hitchhiking, from many months in Iran and I knew he was excited that I was coming home. When I knocked on his study door, he must have been standing almost behind it, for it opened immediately – I would have embraced him as I had learned to do in the Middle East. I would have even settled for his hand – yet his hands were tightly clasped behind his back and his greeting was only a broad smile and "Hello".

We were on our way again, our purpose blessed and confirmed, back up to the ancient track we had been following the day before. We were not stiff from the exercise of the day before, we had been walking all day every day for weeks already. The weather continued hot, dry and sunny. The landscape was changing as we went further into the younger geology of Snowdonia, into ever sharper crags. Far below, on our left, the Traeth Mawr estuary was flat as the sea, green with marshy fields. I had been devouring Tolkien, volume by volume, as Father reviewed first *The Hobbit* and then the three successive volumes of *The Lord of the Rings* and I imbued the cloud-robed crags to the right with goblins, elves and of course, my hero, Strider... I admired Gandalf as well, of course, but more as a father figure – and even Father's beard was not long and white enough for that role.

Ahead and slightly to our right, the great sharp peak of Snowdon itself stood against the sky, the eastern side sharp and craggy, the western rounder, smoother. We even considered walking to the summit (yet again) but decided that we could not get distracted at this point but should press on with our objective. Besides, where could we safely store our packs while we made this diversion? The tree line in North Wales is naturally very low, higher than 200 metres above sea level there are almost no trees, probably because the earth is too shallow at that altitude. Perhaps the tree line was once higher, but when the forests were cut or burned, erosion washed out the earth and new trees could not take hold – much as the Dalmatian coast has been eroded since the woods were cut down to build Venice and its fleets. Homer wrote of Ithaca as a very green and wooded island but that was before the Venetians and goats arrived like locusts, denuding the island, leaving it defenceless against erosion. There are exceptions, such as some sheltered hanging valleys or some government highland plantings of conifers, but in general the mountains are treeless – making for spectacular views, quite unlike the mountains of north-east America, which are so heavily wooded that views are few and far between. The sharp peak of Snowdon, seen from the south, is pure rock and on that side is a sheer cliff that has been used for training for Everest mountaineers. The side flanks of the mountain give way to grass and heather that clothe the rugged slopes in softer forms. Trees only survive down near the bottoms of valleys.

We followed the ancient track over the foot of Cnicht, forded the headwaters of the Afon Dylif at a waterfall that can be seen as a splash of white for miles around... so once again there was a spectacular view down the hills to the coast and Cardigan Bay. Here the slopes were steep, but our track kept to the contours, so the going was easy enough. Then it dropped downhill into ancient natural woods of oak and beech, where we reached a farm track that turned into a single-lane road. Here we changed course from the way I had come on horseback, so as to avoid having to walk along two miles of main road, over the bridge at the Aberglaslyn Pass and up the west bank of the River Glaslyn. Instead, we stayed on the east bank that falls sheer into the water, except that an old, disused narrow-gauge slate railway had been carved into the rock. We could not have taken it with ponies, because it entailed going through a few fairly short tunnels. The roofs of these tunnels dripped constantly, despite the general drought of summer and naturally we went back into Tolkien and threatened each other that: "Gollum is living in here, in this dark, damp tunnel. He'll soon jump out on us, thinking that we're carrying his 'Precious' and tear at our flesh with his filthy claws and rotted teeth." Only much later was I to learn that the mountains and old mines of Wales were indeed an original source of inspiration to the writer.

The ponies may have been terrified by passing buses belching diesel fumes but they certainly would have refused point blank to go into these dark tunnels, Gollum or no.

The pass is spectacular, for the river Glaslyn has carved out a gorge through the mountain and both sides are sheer rock, with a few brave conifers holding on here and there. Besides, we felt infinitely superior walking alone on our side of the river, while tourists in cars and buses were all on the road on the other side. In 1955, there were no rails (they had been salvaged for iron in the War), but today the line has been restored and opened as the Porthmadog-Caernarfon Welsh Highland Railway.

We walked through the tourist town of Beddgelert with its grey stone buildings, hotels and shops. Some time prior to the mid-nineteenth century, a legend was created to attract tourists. George Borrow recounts it in his book *Wild Wales* (1862). In the legend, Prince Llewelyn went out hunting, leaving his baby son in the custody of his faithful dog Gelert. Upon his return, he could not find the child and his dog's muzzle was covered in blood. Mad with rage he killed the faithful hound, but then found his baby son safe and sound – and the corpse of the wolf that Gelert had killed to save him. The Prince buried his dog and you can visit its 'grave' – the 'Grave of Gelert'. Apparently the name Gelert actually comes from St Gelert, a local saint who lived in the sixth century. Living in Wales myself, I felt superior to the tourists who came to 'Ooh and aah' at the magnificent scenery. So we just walked on through the little town without stopping, though Borrow himself said that the Aberglaslyn Pass (the gorge though which we had just walked) rivalled in beauty any such gorge in the Alps or Pyrenees.

We continued along the little disused railway (missing out an annoying loop just upriver from the town) and kept walking until we reached some more government forestation of small pines. On our left rose Moel Hebog at 782 metres and a little further orth was Moel yr Ogof, where there is a cave near the summit in which Owain Glyn Dwr is said to have hidden from the English troops – he had a reputation for disappearing magically whenever necessary and certainly was a survivor. It is known that he lived into his late fifties, no mean feat in those days for a guerrilla fighter, but we could not muster the strength or the enthusiasm to go and visit his cave. By then evening was coming on and we were sufficiently exhausted to call it a day, though with our late start (thanks to oversleeping after Father's curry), we had only covered a dozen miles. Or perhaps our short legs were getting shorter.

So we pitched our little tent near the edge of a forestry project, but far from any habitation, on some poor highland grazing where the sheep were running wild, their owners' marks dyed in their wool until next year's sheering. We cooked up our nondescript fuel of food and collapsed with exhaustion.

XXVI

MERLIN AND OTHER WIZARDS

Now, to our right (looking east), the Snowdonia range looked quite different. We were looking at it from the west side, compared with the view from the south, which was so familiar from home. From this side it is far less craggy, less 'awesome' as eighteenth-century travellers would put it, in fact quite comfortably rounded, its great slopes mostly covered in short grass. The far more dramatic view, the view to which I was so accustomed was of a vast cirque of cliffs, a far more ominous and unwelcoming sight – though also, by far and away, the most exciting. Now we were in a much quieter, more domesticated landscape of great rolling hills rising to unspectacular round summits of 600 metres (1,800 feet).

We awoke early and after some hot chocolate, white bread (all that was available at the time) and jam, we struck camp and started out again. We had a brief argument as to which way was the best to go west from here. Due west was the great round lump of the Mynydds, Mynydd Crib Goch and Mynydd Tal-y-Mignedd, rising to just over 600 metres and 6½ miles long north to south, with hardly a rock to be seen. They really didn't count as 'mountains' to us and anyway, the ups and downs of our last two days' walk carrying packs, had been quite hard enough. The only question was whether to go around them to the south or to the north. I forgot who proposed which, but in the end, we decided it looked more interesting to the north, with its lakes and sparse population.

First we had to walk north past the Mynydds and then we could cut west through a pass. On this third day, time started to melt à la Salvador Dali or as it does on a long ocean crossing. We trudged much of the time with our heads down. The elation of setting out was wearing thin. Our feet hurt, as did our legs, despite being in good training. No doubt we were starting to stink, for the weather kept hot and we sweated profusely. Clothes-washing was not on our agenda. Most of the time I washed my own clothes by hand at home, but it probably took some adult or sibling prodding to do so. They were not around so we ignored our smells. We were probably not even aware of them.

All along our way, there had been markings on the Ordnance Survey maps we carried for 'Burial Mound', 'Stone Circle', 'Camp' or 'Settlement'. None of them had been excavated at the time, so we knew there was nothing to see, except perhaps one or two standing stones, the rest flat on the ground, or for burial mounds and settlements, there would just be a few lumps, covered in grass. Really not 'worth the detour' as the *Guide Michelin* would put it.

I do remember visiting one small archaeological dig in the mountains. I believe I was about ten at the time, but the experience marked me enough to write (at thirteen) my first published work: an article about the myth and the supporting archaeology. It was led by an old family friend called Wilfred Hemp. He generously showed me around, explaining techniques and theories as if I were an adult colleague. The site was the very top of a small, steep hill, a huge rock covered in trees and grass that jutted up in the middle of a deep valley. Legend had it that a British king called Vortigern decided to build a small fortress on the top of this rock, so as to control all traffic through the valley. Each day, his men laid foundations, but by morning they were gone. After several frustrating days like this, he consulted a local sage and was told that there was a curse on the hill and that the only solution was to go to the city of Caernarfon, find an orphan boy and sacrifice the child on the site, spreading his blood liberally on the ground. That, he was assured, would cure the curse.

The king went to Caernarfon himself to find an orphan. He had no trouble doing so amongst the many street urchins running around. He grabbed a likely candidate and brought him back to the building site. Once there, he called the sage to perform the rite and he duly arrived, sharpened knife in hand. All of a sudden, the little boy seemed to change. In a voice of authority, he asked the king why he was being sacrificed; When the king explained the situation, the little boy scoffed at him, saying that his information was false. "The problem," said the little boy, "is that there are two dragons under your building site which are eating your foundations every night. Killing me will not help you one whit. What you need to do is to dig up the dragons, slay them and then you may build your castle in peace." He sounded so convincing that the king had his men dig up the dragons, slew them with his own sword and turned to thank the little boy and to allow him to go back to Caernarfon.

But the urchin was no longer a child, he was the young Wizard Merlin or MyrddinWyllt or also Myrddin Emrys, and he turned to the king saying: "No thank you. This is indeed a fine site and I shall be building my own fort here…" and with a magic wave, the king and his cohorts scattered. Merlin built his own fortress.

From the viewpoint of the builder, the top of a great rock hill should have provided a perfectly sound foundation for a building. What the king did not know, was that many hundreds, perhaps thousands of years before, during the bronze age, some tribe or family group built a large communal hut on top of the hill. The walls were of stone with perhaps mud in between the stones. A rough wooden frame of branches covered with reeds provided a roof with a hole in the middle to let out the smoke. They appeared to have lived there for some time, given the quantity of stone and bronze implements found and the smoke-blackened (but not burned) thatch, but then it was abandoned, probably because of disease or attacks from other tribes. The roof fell in, rotted and the walls (now lined with rotted thatch as well as the mud 'mortar') formed a waterproof cistern or pond. Gradually the pond silted up and 'miraculously' there was a small soft bog right on top of a rocky hill.

The princely builder had no reason to suspect such soft ground, but each time his men laid foundations, they sank into the marshy earth. Thus, the archaeological dig found four layers of foundations laid one upon the other. By then, the foundations had sunk to the bottom of the bog and were stable, which was when the young Merlin was brought on the scene, coincidentally when building could indeed continue successfully. Thus the dig justified the legend, if you accept dragons and wizards as a little poetic licence.

So, unless the sites were excavated, and there are so many of them in Britain it would be an impossible task, there is nothing much to look at. Indeed, in the middle of the city of Chester, you may visit the remains of some Roman baths some two thousand years old. You go into a small fish and chips joint with orange formica tables and moulded plastic chairs, you ask politely for 'The Baths' and a waitress will cheerfully point out a door in the side of the kitchen. As you go through the door, someone may call out: "Watch your head, mate!" The steep steps lead down to a small part of the once opulent Roman baths below the city. So Life goes on.

We continued up the disused slate railway track for a while, then started to work our way west, to the left, on a small path which led up through the Beddgelert woods. We passed to the west of Llyn-y-Gader, a large, cold, very deep lake where we stopped to rest and perhaps wash our faces (but certainly not behind our ears). Then we continued on through the pass between the Mynydd hills, leaving Mynydd Mawr on the right. Now we were on a single-track road, but there was no traffic and we made good progress reaching

Nantlle in the afternoon, before the shops closed so we could buy more cans of baked beans and sausages.

It was hot and the sun was bright. We were coming into calmer, flatter, more domesticated countryside. We cut across country for a while, missing Tal-y-sarn to the north and following footpaths as best we could. Nowadays, there are many more designated footpaths, but then landlords were still holding out with their enclosures, complaining that hikers left gates open so their sheep could escape, besides dropping litter and trampling crops – all bad habits that I had been strictly trained to avoid. The hours melded together and the days became confused as well. From our camp just north of Beddgelert we walked until we saw the sea again, a new sea this time, Caernarfon Bay, with the Irish Sea beyond, but the same salt water that sparkles in the distance on a sunny day. We were looking out across flat farmland and could see the solid square tower of St Beuno's Church in Clynnog Fawr in the distance, not far from the scintillating sea. Tomorrow, we would start to trace the steps of the saints in earnest.

To our left, rose another of these round 'lumps' of hills that we disdained for their lack of crags to climb – Bwlch Mawr. Alan made some remark about 'Big Boobs', but if indeed that was what they were, they'd have been silicone ones to be that steep. We were still too young for such anatomical knowledge.

We found a small woodland and by skirting it, decided on a suitable place to pitch our tent, out of sight of anyone. We could have gone to ask a farmer for permission to camp, but I knew that he might refuse and anyway, we preferred to do our own thing. It seemed more private to camp where we wished: out of sight, out of the minds of others. If they didn't see us, they wouldn't be worrying about us setting fires or dropping litter. So, out of sight, out of mind, it was. The next day, there would be some flattened grass where our tent had been pitched and by the end of the day, the grass would be upright once more. Back to that government minister who told me the purpose of public schools was to teach us how to get away with misdeeds without being caught. We were already working on it.

In the morning, we walked down towards the village, a sleepy little place with little over a hundred inhabitants. On the way, we admired the view of the ocean beyond, sandy coves and fiercely jagged points. The Church of Clynnog (where Saint Beuno was buried) is surprisingly large for such a small village, but then the village was not always so small.

In those days, church doors were left open (even if their silver and vestments were locked away). I remember the cool calm inside the church. I remember the great plain round Romanesque arches that flanked the nave – or could they have been Norman arches, I wonder, with points at the top? Now I am no longer sure. It was all a long time ago and even then, I must have only recently learned to distinguish between the different styles of architecture. I remember the unembellished simplicity of an early church. I have not been back there since. The monastery was founded by St Beuno in the seventh century and subsequently sacked by both Vikings and Normans, so the present church dates from the fifteenth and early sixteenth century. Remains have been found of the original monastery of the seventh century. Inside the church is a large chest with lid, made from a single piece of ash wood, for the collection of alms from pilgrims – the padlock on it dates from about 1600. The chest itself a few hundred years older. I insisted that as pilgrims, from now on, we had to give alms, but Alan said he'd rather spend it on chocolate. I put in a twelve-sided thruppeny piece and I think Alan came up with a tiny farthing (1/4 of a penny) with a perky little wren on the back.

In the tiny village, with its dry stone walls of huge round boulders, there was a small store-cum-post office. Outside stood a bright red public telephone cabin. Was there a hint of homesickness in that memory? I had no one to call. Father had no phone in the old mountain house and I knew not where Mother was. As for Alan, he laughed at my suggestion that he call his Dad in London 'reverse charges'. I seem to remember him saying something about his father "Having better things to do than be bothered by his pip-squeak son". We bought some more baked beans and white bread and perhaps a few eggs. There were slim pickings in those remote village stores that now no longer exist at all.

It was very hot and we were getting more grumpy with each other. Saint Beuno had failed to imbue us with his grace. Alan suggested we spend the day swimming at a beach and then walk 'all night', following a small road. So we walked on a while past pebble beaches and found a cove with a sandy beach instead. That looked more accommodating to us and we dropped our packs and our clothes.

Pickled in salt and still groggy from an afternoon nap, we had a meal and set off along the rocky coast, into the lowering sun. We passed south of another big round hill, Yr Eifl, which has an Iron Age fort on it, that has even been compared to Machu Picchu, but we were not inclined to make any detours for history – we had a task at hand, a goal to reach, a pilgrimage to accomplish. I have since been to Machu Picchu and was disappointed by the ruins – they were no more dramatic than the ruins of workers' cottages by abandoned Welsh mines.

Not a single vehicle passed us on the road as we walked and walked. At least it was cooler now and we were further relieved when the sun actually set. What we had not bargained for was the lack of moon. It must have risen much later than the night I had salvaged the 'Flying Dutchman'. It was pitch black, though we could divine the road by the huge looming shadows of the dry stone walls on either side. From time to time we would come to a crossroads and have to consult our map by the failing light of our small flashlight. Trying to see the road signs was even harder and once or twice, Alan hoisted me on his shoulders so that I could feel the raised letters of the cast-iron road signs. As I dictated the double 'L's and 'Y's and double 'D's, Alan cursed the Welsh language until he dropped me from his shoulders, exhausted. By then, he'd had enough of names like: Tyddyn Uchaf, Garnfadryn, Llaniestyn and Meyllteyrn.

Finally, we could walk no further and decided to camp for the night. Neither of us had a watch, so it could have been between midnight and three in the morning. The moon had still not risen and once we had found a gap in the walls, we literally felt our way with our hands. The grass was short here, no doubt heavily grazed by sheep. The ground was surprisingly level and apparently devoid of cowpats. We pitched the tent easily. By now, we could have done it with our hands tied behind our backs. Sleep came like a mugging from behind.

"Cor blimey! What yer nippers doing in mi' garden?" Yelled a puce-red face through the parted flaps of our tent.

"Oh, sir, we're frightfully sorry, sir. We really couldn't see it was private property, sir. We couldn't see anything in the dark, sir." We pacified him with our stuttered apologies until he said he would go and talk it over with the Missus. We could tell from his accent that he was no local – probably a retired man from the Midlands and he could tell from ours that we were no local ragamuffins, but 'toff tramps'. Such was the class distinction set by accent, usually defined by whether or not one's parents could afford to pay for a private education.

We peered outside our tent and saw the extent of our error: we were camped in the middle of a very small, immaculately tended lawn. Luckily we had not come through the flower beds of roses and hollyhocks, nor abused the plaster gnomes, mushrooms and fauns. The house was a neat little brick bungalow such as retired couples from England liked to build for themselves in Wales. We were trying to get dressed inside the tent (never an easy task, given its tiny dimensions) when the owner returned with a tray laden with mugs of tea and plates of good greasy breakfast food. He just admonished us to "Tidy up them tent-peg holes and not to leave any litter." We knew all about that and didn't need the advice, but meekly nodded "Yes sir, no sir," and then added, when he left: "My big toe, sir."

That day, we decided to shorten our walk by trying to get a boat from Abersoch and save ourselves nine or ten miles walking, so we cut back south across the Lleyn Peninsula (much narrower here). Here, the land was flatter, more domesticated. Though still not rich land, fields were enclosed by dry stone walls so it was well nigh impossible to walk off road. We chose the smallest lanes that followed the boundaries of fields. The heat of the last few days had abated and walking faster was no longer such an ordeal.

We reached the small fishing port of Abersoch in the late afternoon. We asked on the pier if any boats would be going to Bardsey Island next day. There was none. Our hearts fell. Everyone said the usual boat went out from Aberdaron and we had better continue on to there. Tired, depressed and discouraged, we could not face walking further that night, so we decided to just sleep on the beach. We did not pitch our tent, but slept on the sand next to the pier. I forget what we ate, but it was certainly not fish and chips from the shop on the front, whose neon lights bothered us all night. Somehow, neither of us was used to the idea of 'going to a restaurant', even if it was a cheap take-out like that. It just seemed too lavish.

Oh yes, in my second school in London where I had met Alan in the first place, there had been a few boys who wore glasses and were continuously teased for excelling in class. Some of them celebrated their birthdays in glitzy restaurants and invited all their tormenting classmates to join them. I admired their academic success and anyway was not inclined to tease them, on the principle of 'people who live in glass houses shouldn't throw stones'. I suppose they were the sons of some of those lucky Jewish families to have reached London before the Nazis got to them. So yes, I had been to restaurants, but certainly never on my dime. That would come much later, when I was earning my own living.

XXVII

PASSAGE TO BARDSEY

In the morning, we hoisted our packs once more and set off down narrow twisting lanes towards our next great hope for a ferry. By now, we were not talking much at all and just kept walking silently, determinedly towards our arbitrary destination. As we stumbled along, we wondered what fool idea we had had, that we should walk to Bardsey in the first place? So, I had come up with the idea, but it was just an idea and then Father had confirmed it and it was sort of all signed and sealed. We were regretting it and here we were, within a few miles of a boat ride to our final destination. We could hardly stop now. Each of us worried what the other one would think if we voiced our exhaustion and need to quit at this point. Besides, where would we go – back to Father in Parc? We knew he did not have time for us. Back to the one-room cottage on the beach? To do what? Of course, we still had money, so we just kept on plodding, one foot in front of the other, again and again. There were no more mountains, not even big round boob ones, just a sight of the sea and the rocky coast to our left. At least it was not so hot any more, we could walk all day until we just dropped from exhaustion. We did stop from time to time to sprawl in a field by the roadside, perhaps to sleep a little. So near to our goal, we were becoming depressed with fatigue.

Finally, in mid-afternoon, we looked down onto the tiny hamlet of Aberdaron, mostly one big hotel right in the middle of the sandy bay. In the year 1115, a local Welsh prince, fleeing from the troops of Henry I of England took refuge in the church here. When the English troops arrived to break the sacred law of 'Refuge in a Sanctuary' by dragging out the prince, they were 'repelled by the local clergy'! Tough vicars they had in those days! Later he escaped to Ireland in a boat belonging to the local monastery.

Now we wondered if there was going to be a boat out from here for us. If there was not, this was the end of the line. There was no further hope of a ferry. We could see no real pier, no protected harbour. Where was a boat to go out from? Once down in the hamlet, the hotel looked far too large and grand for us to dare to enter and enquire about boats but a little past the great edifice there was a tiny cottage with a sign announcing that it was called 'Y Gegin Fawr' (The Big Kitchen), the last place where pilgrims to Bardsey might get a meal ever since the thirteenth century – though they might have to wait for weeks to get safe passage across the perilous straits. This was not encouraging news for us. There seemed to be two minuscule rooms with very low ceilings on the ground floor and two above. We knocked and a little old lady came to the door – "A witch" muttered Alan. If she was so, she was kind enough and told us her nephew would probably be leaving next morning with the tide, about 8 o'clock from Porth Meudwy, a little over a mile further on around the cove. We thanked her and asked her to tell him we'd be there waiting.

"Mind you, young men, if the weather comes up, he won't be going at all. It does that all the time, you just never know," she said as we started off again.

The fields around were so small and neatly mown by sheep, we decided to sleep on the beach once more. No-one could complain about us there. Though the heat wave had broken, it was still clear and sunny. It would not be very down by the water. In the end, we finished up almost the big hotel, but we were out of sight in a little cleft rocks. Once again, we cooked up some fuel, slid into our sleeping bags and slept as if we were at our journey's end.

Next day, there was a good breeze blowing, waves were breaking on the protected beach. Whitecaps shone in the sun, so it was blowing over fifteen knots. We prayed the boat would still be going and hurried around the cliff line to Port Meudwy. The open fishing boat we were to take was bouncing up and down on the leeside of the little pier and we were the first passengers to arrive. Being young boys, of course, we took over the bow thwart and put our packs underneath it. The wettest seat on the boat, but 'we would get there first'!

As we waited for the others to arrive, we discussed camping on Bardsey with the skipper. He told us that the owner did not allow any camping and that we would soon be run off the island if we tried. He did give us a good suggestion, though: he said there was a bird observatory in an old farmhouse on the hill, which had been set up a couple of years before, and that they had quite a few bunks where we might be able to sleep.

He also went on to tell us about the Kings of Bardsey. When the Barons of Newborough owned the island, they started crowning a King, the first being a John Williams in 1826. Another, John Williams II, was deposed in 1900 for alcoholism. The last, a John Pritchard, was outraged when he offered his services and the services of his subjects, at the outset of World War One in 1914 – and was refused, because he was already 71 years old. Disillusioned, he finally left the island in 1925 and died a year later. Perhaps it was about then that my own Father was asked if he would like to be King... although the duties were slight, the prospect of being obliged to spend most of his time on the island discouraged him and he declined.

One of the Newboroughs decided to rebuild the farmhouses and amused himself by building several pebbledash farm cottages on the island, all as attached pairs, with common outbuildings around a courtyard. When he died, he had meticulously left every pair of cottages to two different people whom he knew could not abide each other. He had designed a miniature Hell on his tiny, harbourless island with the idea that everyone would kill their neighbours when the wind came up and they could not get back to the mainland. The legatees were smarter than that and quickly sorted out the mess of their tenancies by swapping the properties, until there was some harmony on the island again.

In 1875, the Estate had offered the islanders either a harbour with a small jetty or a place of worship – they opted for a Methodist chapel, which was probably turned into a school thirty years later. Anyway, there still is no harbour or jetty of any kind.

Finally the other passengers arrived (they were all intending to return that afternoon) and we set off with the old inboard engine chugging away noisily. Bardsey seemed a good way off, though in fact it is only 1.9 miles from land and 5½ from Aberdaron itself. The crossing would take an hour and a half. It is an island just a mile long by 0.6 miles wide, two-thirds of it a steep little hill adequate for sheep grazing, the rest, land flat enough for cows and some poor arable land. There is also a rocky spit with a great lighthouse on the end – the one Father had told us about over our curry dinner together at Parc.

I have never been back, but in those days, there was no jetty or anchorage of any kind. Boats like ours came alongside some sharp rocks on which our skipper stood and held onto his bucking boat as passengers fell ashore. As we started off with our packs, he said he would be leaving that afternoon or would be back in a few days to take us back, so if it was not that day, he'd take us off soon enough. Little did we know just how long we would be staying…

Our first priority was to find out if indeed we could stay at the newly-created bird observatory, in a farmhouse called 'Cristin'. Enquiries pointed us in the direction of a farmhouse larger than the others, built on the flanks of the hill (to spare flat land for farming) and with several large outbuildings. In my memory they were built of corrugated iron. The administrator was a wiry little man called Roy or something, with those unflinching, unblinking, piercing yellow-gold eyes of a bird of prey. He said we would have to pay for our bunks and food and work for the bird observatory as well – the other occupants were mostly university students interested in birds and a cheap summer holiday. When I pointed out that we did not have enough to pay for more than a night or two, he said he would settle up with my Parents. So we moved in.

XXVIII

STORM BOUND

That night the weather changed. The wind came up and any idea of going back to the mainland was on hold, 'at the pleasure of the Almighty'.

We slipped easily into the routine of mess meals (though no one trusted us with cooking), dishwashing duties, housework duties and above all bird duties. In the evenings, we sat around and our learned elders played guessing games about birds, one person writing down a specific bird, the rest guessing species, genus, family and so on until they found the bird. We often crawled off to bed before the game was over.

Around midnight or 2 am, if conditions were right, we would be rousted out of bed to collect migrating birds. Most birds cannot land in the dark, so when they are migrating for huge distances, they sometimes just fall, exhausted, into the sea. But a lighthouse beam that sweeps the side of a hill provides the perfect solution: for moments at a time, they can actually see where to land and land they do. Unfortunately they also tend to fly straight into the lighthouse. There are over 1,000 casualties a year on the Bardsey Light. They fall sound asleep with exhaustion just as we two little boys would after walking all day in the heat, with packs on our backs. We would take two-wheeled wheelbarrows out into the night with flashlights and literally sweep up the exhausted creatures, great and small, in our arms and dump them in the barrows.

Back at the observatory, there was a huge wire-netting

cage into which we could empty them, checking to remove any raptors and taking those straight into the ringing barn to be processed at once and released. The harmless little fellows could wait until morning to be sent on their way. Being so young, we would be sent back to bed as soon as the big rush was over, but after breakfast, we would be back out there. Either we would help ring birds – I can still feel the thrill of holding a tiny goldcrest in my hand (the smallest bird in Europe at about 5 grams!), its back in my palm, its neck between my forefinger and second finger, one tiny ankle between my thumb and little finger, so I could snap on a miniscule numbered ring with my free hand. An adult would record the data and if it flew away of its own accord, that was fine, but usually they had to be taken out to the grass to go on sleeping. It was if we were operating on them under anaesthetic. Once they had recuperated, they would be off again.

Oh, the magic of holding such a tiny creature, a sentient living thing, so complete with brain, heart, lungs, liver and all the rest, in the palm of my hand. Already, I found the workings of a tiny wristwatch both fascinating and magical, but this was truly miraculous – and we were surrounded by millions of these miracles.

On the wall of the barn was a detailed map of the island, with land clearly marked that was "out-of-bounds" to us because the farmers didn't trust us to close the gates and so on – besides a huge world map with hundreds of coloured pins denoting where 'our' birds had been observed, dead or alive. All of this information (on some 8,000 birds ringed here a year) was being compiled to increase our knowledge of migration, the state of the bird kingdom and how they may be protected. There were many choughs (a kind of crow, pitch black but with bright orange legs and beak, it is related to the jackdaw), wheateaters, sedge warblers, whitethroats and spotted fly catchers.

During daylight, we might be sent off to observe waders on the beach, armed with a notebook, pencil and binoculars.

We were strictly told never to take a bird book with us, lest we imagine traits that we could not see, but fitted a bird on a page. We were told to make detailed notes of what we actually saw and come back to have it identified in a scientific, unbiased situation.

Alan was usually sent to the northern escarpment of the hill, where it dropped so suddenly into the sea. There, he studied and noted the nesting shearwaters. I, on the other hand, was usually sent to the beach to study waders. The beach had no bluff above it, so it involved wriggling flatter than an infantryman – memories of the air-gun battles on Hampstead Heath, came back to me though now knowing that there was no one out there to take a pot shot at me! I would stop in the very last of the beach grass, just before it became pure sand, and lie motionless for what seemed like hours. Either the oystercatchers and curlews hadn't seen me or perhaps they considered that I was no threat. But the seals always became inquisitive and would come flumping up the beach towards me, on their flippers, to study me with their quizzical little eyes and lively nostrils, their long whiskers twitching. I often wondered if they went home to study our own species in seaweed tomes below the waves.

While the whole island was honeycombed with rabbit warrens (this was before myxomatosis) many of the burrows had been taken over by Manx sheerwaters. On dark, moonless nights, there was a sinister cackling all around from these 7,000 nesting sheerwaters, along with razorbills, guille-mots, fulmars and kittiwakes. One great advantage to nesting on this island is that there are no predators, such as rats or foxes, so they may raise their families in relative peace.

Sheerwaters regularly fly across the Atlantic to South America. They lay one egg a year but only sit on that at night for fear that animals will find their precious egg if they are seen going to it by day. An experiment was conducted on their navigation systems: at migration time they were taken to New York by ship and their 'clocks' readjusted by turning on lights and playing recordings of sheerwaters feeding at calculated, incorrect times. Released at their destination, they all spiralled up high in the sky and set off in exactly the 'right' wrong direction to reach Brazil. Alas, at that time, transmitters were not made small enough for them to be tagged with one, so no one knows if they ever made it, or how long it took to understand their error and redirect their flight. They are known to live for 55 years and more, so the one egg a year rhythm does not endanger their species. They are very different from their cousins of the same genus, the puffin. While sheerwaters do a great deal of quite leisurely gliding and swooping to cover their 10,000 kilometres a year, puffins' wings beat at 400 times a minute. Their wings are so small that they are unable to take off from calm water. They need waves to jump off and become airlifted. So they do not go far afield.

I still say 'we', but somewhere along the line, on that tiny island, Alan and I had drifted apart and we rarely did anything together any more. Being trapped on an island has the effect of a pressure cooker: however delightful the island and the circumstances, the very idea that you cannot leave, even if you don't want to at that time, is enough to serve as the grain of sand in the oyster, an irritant that gets in the way of complete enjoyment and certainly in the way of friendship. Many years later, my first wife and I flew from Venezuela to San Andreas with the hope of flying on from there to Costa Rica, where we had left our decrepit car (bought in New York for $200). San Andreas is one of the most idyllic little coral atoll islands in the Caribbean – that limpid blue sea, so transparent you can see the bigger fish by the coral reefs as you fly in. There were no grand hotels there at the time. We spent the night in our hammock between two coconut trees on the beach. We longed to snorkel the reefs. Yet on arrival, we had been told there were no empty seats out for three weeks – and we had a rendezvous in Guatemala City in a few days. We were not to know that our friend would show up 24 hours late

– because he had found "a memorable whore house" in town! So instead of relaxing and enjoying this fabulous island, next morning we went at once to the airfield and sat on our packs, waiting for standby seats. As it turned out, we got on the very first flight out. That was almost forty years ago. I have never been back. I am afraid of what change will have come by now: luxury hotels, crowds, drugs and crime. I have already seen enough of that elsewhere.

So it was that we both waited, as we worked, for news of the first boat back. The strong winds and heavy seas continued day after day. There was no telephone on the island except the radio in the lighthouse, and that was for emergency use only. Our parents had no news of us, there was no way to get any to them. A few years later, one of the two lighthouse keepers became disturbed and hacked his colleague apart with an axe. Soon after that, one of the bird wardens also went 'funny' and had to be taken away in a straitjacket. In both cases, I wonder how news was sent to the police. Perhaps such incidents did indeed qualify as 'emergencies'. I can just see the struggling men, bound in white canvas, being passed from the jagged rocks into the bouncing cork of a little fishing boat…

The lighthouse intrigued us, but it was out of bounds and we were too timid to try and meet the keepers. It was square and had been built in 1821, to guide shipping from the St George's Channel out into the Irish Sea. Apparently, it was only converted to electricity in 1973 – by which time I was far away in South America. So when I was there it was still running on kerosene and needed to be staffed full-time.

We did not go crazy. We were not old enough for that. We just went silent… and silently, perhaps sullenly, went about our tasks.

Eventually, there was little food left on the island. Alan and I were so hungry that once, when no one else was around, we crept into the food store and stole a slice of white bread each, which we covered with marmalade and devoured voraciously. The theft has weighed upon my conscience these fifty-five years and more...

Then Roy, the warden, announced that we had a whole leg of lamb killed by one of the farmers that very morning. We roasted it and ate it, though the grown-ups complained that it tasted strange, being so fresh and not hung. Personally, I was hungry enough to enjoy every morsel. Beggars can't be choosers and when you're hungry, you're hungry... nowadays I don't eat meat any more. Back in that situation, with no food, I would gladly eat meat again.

Our duties did not take up all our time and we often went walking alone, each in his own direction and taken up with his own thoughts. I remember particularly enjoying the view from the top of the bare hill. Though only 548 feet high, the panoramic, windswept scene was wonderful from there. There were very few trees and those that existed were stunted to the size of large bushes. To the northeast, the ground fell away steeply to the rocky coast. Southwest the slope was more gentle and levelled out to the skirt of flat land on which stood the few vestiges of the ruined monastery. It had been built by Saint Cadfan (who was from Brittany) in the year 516. I do not envy his journey all the way to North Wales, no doubt in some form of coracle or other animal skin-covered frame. It is some 300 miles directly by sea, and one can be sure that he was often blown off course and had to seek food and water on land. I have covered such a distance in an open ship's lifeboat, fitted with pre-Homeric rigging – but at least that was a sturdy, unsinkable hull, not a light wicker frame covered with oiled or tarred animal skins!

Down there, twenty thousand saints were said to be buried but the earth is so shallow, before hitting rock, I wondered if the saints had not found their eternal resting place in the waves, rather than in the ground. They say there is deeper earth near the still-standing tower of the monastery and there is a cross, dating from the sixth century. In 584, Saint Deiniol (Bishop of Bangor) was buried there, as was

Saint Dyfrig (though he was moved to the Cathedral of Llandaff in 1120). By the year 1212, it had become a regular pilgrimage destination, termed: 'Canons Regular', and three pilgrimages to Bardsey were considered worth one to Rome, not, as Father thought, to Jerusalem. In 1284, Edward I made a pilgrimage there. The deeper earth could have been an inlet, then a lake at one time, which has since silted up and become soft ground, suitable for burial… or indeed, cultivation. There, the saints could have been buried, one above the other. As for the exact number, I am sure that distant history is full of poetic licence or plain exaggeration. Of course the monastery (like most of the others in Britain) was destroyed on the orders of Henry VIII, with Dissolution and the Reformation.

We probably only stayed a couple of weeks on Bardsey Island, but to our childish minds, it went on forever without beginning or end. A period of indefinite length, suspended in time. Then, quite suddenly, one day we were back sitting on the bow thwart of the little fishing boat, heading for Aberdaron and 'civilization' (such as fish and chips). With our friendship chilled and our psyches exhausted, we decided to hightail it home. The bishop would have left by now and we could each have our own bedroom again. We did not even discuss walking all the way. We were wiped out. We hitchhiked instead.

XXIX

HOME AT LAST

Seven miles from home, we were dropped in Maentwrog and I finally went to a public telephone and called home, reversing the charges. Father answered and accepted the call. He expressed no surprise that we were still alive, nor even that we were finally coming home. He just said: "Good. Stay right there. We're going out to dinner with Hamish and his wife. We'll pick you up on the way through."

Sure enough, half an hour later, the rattling old grey jeep pulled up with my Parents. We climbed into the back with our packs and set off up into the mountains, high up behind Llan Ffestiniog. In its heyday around 1900, it was a flourishing slate-mining town, but by the end of the War the slate business was no longer viable and many houses looked abandoned, with broken window panes and front doors hanging askew – but the truth was that unemployment was as high as 46 per cent and those who had not left, had given up hope. Already, by 1955, there were a few small signs of revival, but it was still a blighted slate town. It would take years before some slate mines would be reopened as tourist attractions. The main road through Ffestiniog was asphalt with just enough width to pass an oncoming bus or truck.

Then we took a single-track asphalt road much higher into the mountains. After a while, there was a rocky track up to the right and at the top of that track stood Hamish's hafod, or highland farm.

The house had once been a retreat for monks and also a place for them to tend their sheep on the summer pastures. It was a low stone farmhouse with a tiny chapel attached. All around were rocks with patches of grass in between. Stone walls had been built to clear rocks from the grass, but it was still a very poor little hill farm. The house and chapel certainly predated the Reformation, so they were over 400 years old.

Hamish and his wife, Daphne, were English (well, he was Scottish, but just as much an outsider) and had two small children. She was fragile and lithe, a dancer, if I remember correctly. He was a short little squat bull of a rugby-playing man who never did anything at a walk – he sprinted from his workbench to the car he was working on, from table to sink with the dirty dishes. He had red hair and a most combative nature, especially after 'having drink taken'. A mechanical genius, he had driven a 1913 Lagonda motor car from London to Cape Town and now restored other vintage cars. He had converted the tiny chapel into his garage. He put a wide door in the west wall and had enough space for two cars side by side. He used the altar as his workbench, his tools hung neatly on the east wall in place of a crucifix. At that time, he was working on a 1928 supercharged Alfa Romeo (a bright red two-seater) and a 1924 four-seater OM touring car, both Italian marques. In the old cow barns he had a few early Bugattis (some with the pointed 'boat tail' of the 1920s) that he not only raced, but to the scandal of vintage car collectors, even drove (rather than bringing them on a trailer) all the way to and from the race track: over 200 miles each way to Silverstone, in a one or two-seater priceless antique car with only rear-wheel brakes.

He once took me for a drive in a two-seater 1920 Bugatti Brescia. The seats were of cane work, the passenger sitting a little further back than the driver, so his legs lay beside the driver's seat. My job was to pump up the pressure on the cylindrical petrol tank behind me (this one was earlier and did not sport the boat tail) to maintain fuel supply to the carburettor. The mudguards were of shining copper, the paintwork in bright Bugatti blue and the 1.4 litre four-cylinder, sixteen-valve engine growled and howled. We roared off further up into the mountains on the one-track asphalt road, taking the sharp turns at the speed only a practised racing car driver can pull off successfully. I kept thinking of that photograph Hamish had, framed from a press shot of him racing at Silverstone, taking a corner on two wheels, the other two flying so high you could see the crowd beyond under the tyres. Then suddenly we stopped. Something was severely amiss. Our roaring élan was aborted. We were not on an even keel. One back wheel had fallen off, the centre lock hub had stripped its thread. We trotted back home…

Needless to say, as a young boy I worshipped him. His drunken eccentricities were not my problem – his cars and his enthusiasm were my joy. As for my Parents, they were intrigued by this attractive, eccentric young couple (whose palpable mutual attraction was fiercely magnetic) and their arrival to the neighbourhood… though their sympathies later went to his (by then) abused wife.

I assume we were both carried out to the Jeep after dinner. I have no memory of our departure. Later, Mother remarked only that she had never seen two such filthy dirty little boys as we, when they picked us up. Not in Tangier, nor Naples, nor in the slums of Liverpool. I shall never know if, in fact, she was anxious when I was away with Alan for so long without communication, or if she was satisfied that we were sensible enough and could cope alone. Life in general and communications in particular were so very different then.

Was this, then, the great 'eureka' moment? Did this truly mean that henceforth I could just get up and walk to Kabul or Tokyo? Not exactly, but now my foot was in the door and I had been introduced to the concept that the world could be my stomping ground… you, the reader, may see this as the End. For me, it was only the Beginning.

AFTERWORD

How Parents raise their children certainly went through a sea-change after May 25th, 1979.

On that day, a six-year-old boy was walking to the school bus two blocks from his parents' loft in Soho, New York. For the first time he was, very proudly, alone. He had been trying to persuade his parents to let him walk to the bus alone and had just received the green light. He disappeared without trace. His elfin smile became famous, it was printed on milk cartons all over America. The search was intense. His name was Etan Patz.

The chief suspect was a kind and gentle African American odd-job man named Othneil Miller. He had done some work for us and for the Patzes. More than thirty years later, another man confessed and, as I write, is standing trial. Poor Othneil must have suffered hell all that time, his life in tatters knowing that he was innocent and his gentle character besmirched.

So it was that I could not dispute the paranoia of my children's mother – for an absurdly long time, one of us would take them to school and pick them up. They were not even allowed to take the school bus until they were too old to be allowed to take it! They have, of course, since declared their freedom with many adventurous journeys in more or less arduous conditions and successfully negotiated the perils of nature and man... coming home intact, wiser and more developed in every way.

It is debatable as to whether there are more or fewer tragic disappearances today than when I was a child, or even a hundred years ago – what is certain, is that modern media (now even using milk cartons) has made us all much more aware of such dangers. I doubt that there is any more or less pederasty today than in the past. I do know that if a child spoke to their parents of abuse, that frequently they might be shushed-up, "it's in your mind", "…such a respectable person", "wouldn't ever do such a thing". Nowadays, they are more likely to be heard out.

On the one hand, one might conjecture that the 'sexual liberation' movement could defuse sexual frustration and thus reduce abuse. On the other, perhaps permissiveness breaks down any social inhibitions.

I shall leave that debate to sociologists and only say that, despite the pain and anguish, I suffered an amazing child-hood, which would not be easy to duplicate today – any more than Tom Sawyer might be reincarnated.

ACKNOWLEDGEMENTS

I would like to acknowledge and thank all those who helped in this modest endeavour. My Parents who gave me this life, this view, these strange tools with which to stay afloat. My wife, Kimberly for her editorial skills, besides ferociously seeing off those 'black dogs' that haunt any writer, trying to sabotage the very muse that actually does the writing. My oldest friend, Alan Trist, who I have recovered after so many years and who has edited my story and his. My siblings, for their lack of objections to the story – which I take as accept-ance, besides correcting my dormant Welsh. For the kind and most professional editorial assistance from my nephew Dominic Wells and sister-in-law Ginnie Goff Greene. Besides encouragement from Jeannette Seaver (Arcade Publishing), Peter Blegvad, Mark Ellingham (Sort of Books), Richard Poole (for 'helicopter parents'). And of course, Mick Felton (Seren) for providing this small tale of life in Wales with book form.

THE AUTHOR

Owain Hughes (born 1943) was educated at Shrewsbury School and Keble College, Oxford. All his life he has travelled world-wide, usually on the ground or by sea, rarely by air. He worked in Market Research for a Nationalised Steel Company in London, taught English in Iran, worked as electrician for a kinetic sculptor in Paris, then in Osaka, Japan. He wrote about North Africa, crossed Russia by train, scoured the whole of Latin America, sailed the European and East Coast American seas, both cruising and racing. Author of two novels, he now lives in New York and Mexico.

SEREN

Well chosen words

Seren is an independent publisher with a wide-ranging list which includes poetry, fiction, biography, art, translation, criticism and hstory. many of our authors have been on longlists and shortlists – and have won – major literary prizes. among them the Costa Award, the Man Booker, the Desmond Elliott Prize, the Ondaatje Prize, the Writers' Guild Award, the Forward Prize and the T.S. Eliot Prize.

At the heart of our list is a good story told well or an idea or history presented interestingy or provocatively. We're international in authorship and readership though our roots are here in Wales (Seren means Star in Welsh), where we prove that writers from a small country with an intricate culture have a worldwide relevance.

Our aim is to publish work of the highest literary and artistic merit that also succeeds commercially in a competitive, fast-changing environmet. You can help us achieve this goal by reading more of our books – available from all good bookshops and increasingly as e-books. You can also buy them at a 20% discount from our website, and get updates about forthcoming titles, readings, launches and other news about Seren and the authors we publish.

www.serenbooks.com